Queen Elizabeth the QUEEN MOTHER

Written and Edited by Douglas Keay

Published by IPC Magazines Limited,
King's Reach Tower,
Stamford Street, London SE1 9LS
at the recommended price
shown on the frontispiece

Printed in England by Jarrold and Sons Limited,
Whitefriars, Norwich NR3 1SH

ISBN 85037 516 9

© IPC MAGAZINES Limited 1980

£2.25

Production Editors   Tony Skudder, Art
Jean Elgie, Editorial

Art Editor   Jack Clare

Layout Artist   Malcolm Harwood

Editorial Research   Rosalind Bateman

Picture Research   Brian Mumford
Percy Hatchman

Picture Editor   Dennis Beaven

Publisher   Jane Reed

Cover   John Shelley/OPFA

Contents

To HM Queen Elizabeth the Queen Mother,
from John Brooke-Little MVO, Richmond Herald of Arms

Ma'am, it is very hard to believe that 80 summers have passed since you
were born. For 24 years I have been an Officer of Arms, helping to arrange and
take part in the great ceremonies of state, and so have stood on the touch-line
watching the phenomenon of a changeless Queen. It has been a wonderful
experience and a great privilege.

You have sailed through the first 80 years of your life, many of them
turbulent years, radiating serenity, infinite charm and amazing good humour.
You have been a source of comfort and inspiration to countless thousands,
performing your many tasks with love and for love. If you have ever felt weary
and under the weather, and in the nature of things you must have, I can
honestly say that I have never noticed it; your friendliness and warm smile are
ever present.

Thank you Ma'am for giving so much of yourself to so many for so long.
In all you have done you have strayed far beyond the call of duty, but this, I
assure you, has never been in vain nor gone unnoticed. I would like to think
that you might now take a well-earned rest. I am afraid this is a vain hope, but
at least do sit back and enjoy your birthday year, bathed in the warm sunshine
of the love and gratitude of your innumerable admirers. May God bless you
and grant you many more years of happiness.

John Brooke-Little
Richmond

Orders, honours and tours

Orders of Chivalry
Lady of the Most Noble Order of the Garter
Lady of the Most Ancient and Most Noble Order of the Thistle
Lady of the Imperial Order of the Crown of India
Grand Master and Dame Grand Cross of the Royal Victorian Order
Dame Grand Cross of the Most Excellent Order of the British Empire
Dame Grand Cross of the Venerable Order of St. John of Jerusalem
Royal Victorian Chain
Grand Cross of the Legion of Honour
Grand Cross of the Order of the Lion of the Netherlands
Grand Cross of the Order of the Crown of Roumania
Grand Cross of St. Olga and St. Sophia of Greece
Grand Cross of the Order of St. Sava of Serbia
Grand Cross of the Order of Lernor Ala of Afghanistan
Grand Cross of the Order of the Sun of Peru
Grand Cross of the Order of Independence of the Republic of Tunisia
Member of the Order of Ojaswi Rajanya of Nepal

Honours
Her Majesty Queen Elizabeth the Queen Mother was appointed the
Lord Warden and Admiral of the Cinque Ports and Constable of
Dover Castle in September 1978

Chancellor of the University of London

Honorary Degrees (Doctor of Laws): Queen's University,
     Belfast
     St. Andrews
     Glasgow
     Edinburgh
     Cape Town
     Cambridge
     Manchester
     Leeds
     Columbia, New York
     Melbourne
     Liverpool
     Auckland, New Zealand
     Dalhousie University,
     Halifax, Nova Scotia
     Dundee
(Doctor of Civil Law): Oxford
(Doctor of Literature): London
     West Indies
     Keele
(Doctor of Music): Sheffield

Honorary Fellow: University College, London
     King's College, London
     Royal College of Obstetricians and
     Gynaecologists
     Royal College of Physicians, London
     Royal College of Physicians of Edinburgh
     Royal College of Surgeons of England
Royal Fellow: Society of Antiquaries, London
Fellow: Royal Society

President: University College of Rhodesia and Nyasaland
     Royal College of Music
     British Red Cross Society (1937–52, now
     Deputy President)
     National Trust
Grand President: Victorian Order for Nurses for Canada

Bencher of the Middle Temple

Honorary Freeman of the Worshipful Companies of:
Grocers
Merchant Taylors
Barbers
Shipwrights
Musicians

Honorary member of Lloyds

Medals: Gold Albert Medal of the Royal Society of Arts
     French Red Cross Medal
     Norwegian War Cross

Colonel-in-Chief:	1st Queen's Dragoon Guards
	Queen's Own Hussars
	9/12th Royal Lancers (Prince of Wales's)
	King's Regiment
	Royal Anglian Regiment
	Black Watch (Royal Highland Regiment)
	Light Infantry
	Royal Army Medical Corps
	Black Watch (Royal Highland Regiment) of Canada
	Toronto Scottish Regiment
	Royal Australian Army Medical Corps
	Royal New Zealand Army Medical Corps
	Canadian Forces Medical Services

Honorary Colonel:	Royal Yeomanry
	London Scottish (Gordon Highlanders)
	University of London Contingent Officers' Training Corps

Commandant-in-Chief:	Royal Air Force Central Flying School
	Women's Royal Naval Service
	Women's Royal Army Corps
	Women's Royal Air Force
	Nursing Corps and Divisions of St. John Ambulance Brigade

Air Chief Commandant: Women's Royal Australian Air Force

Her Majesty Queen Elizabeth the Queen Mother has received the Freedom of:

Glasgow
Stirling
Dunfermline
Perth
Edinburgh
Inverness
City of London
King's Lynn
Dundee
Forfar
Musselburgh
Wick
Aberdeen
St. Albans

The overseas tours of the Queen Mother

1953	Southern Rhodesia
1954	The United States and Canada
1956	France
1957	The Federation of Rhodesia and Nyasaland
1958	Canada, Honolulu, Fiji, New Zealand, Australia, Mauritius, Uganda, Malta
1959	Kenya and Uganda
	Italy and France—in Italy she visited the Pope in Rome
1960	The Federation of Rhodesia and Nyasaland
1961	Tunisia
1962	Canada
1963	France
1964	The Caribbean
1965	Jamaica
	France
	Canada
	Germany
1966	Canada, Honolulu, Fiji, Australia and New Zealand
1967	France
	Canada
1968	Denmark
1974	Canada
1975	Iran and Cyprus
1976	France
1979	Canada

Prince
Andrew
(1960–)

Prince
Edward
(1964–)

Master Peter
Phillips
(1977–)

David,
Viscount
Linley
(1961–)

Lady Sarah
Armstrong-
Jones
(1964–)

Prince
Charles
(1948–)

Capt. Mark Phillips m. Princess
Anne (b. 1950–)

Antony, Earl of Snowdon m. Princess
Margaret (b. 1930–)

Queen Elizabeth II (1926–)
Reign 1952–
m. Philip, Duke of Edinburgh (1921–)

King George VI (1895–1952)
Reigned 1936–1952
m. Lady Elizabeth Bowes-Lyon
(1900–)

Michael
Bowes-Lyon
(1893–1953)

David
Bowes-Lyon
(1902–1961)

George, Duke of Kent
(1902–1942) m. Princess Marina
of Greece

Prince John
(1905–1919)

Fergus
Bowes-Lyon
(1889–1915)

Rose Bowes-
Lyon
(1890–1967)

Patrick
Bowes-Lyon
(1884–1949)

Henry, Duke
of Gloucester
(1900–1974)

Mary,
Princess
Royal
(1897–1965)

King Edward VIII (1894–1972)
Reigned Jan.–Dec. 1936
m. Mrs Wallis Warfield

Alexander
Bowes-Lyon
(1887–1911)

John
Bowes-Lyon
(1886–1930)

Mary Bowes-
Lyon
(1883–1961)

King George V (1865–1936)
Reigned 1910–1936
m. Princess Mary of Teck
(1867–1953)

Claude, 14th Earl of Strathmore
(1855–1944) m. Nina Cecilia
Cavendish-Bentinck
(1862–1938)

Saturday's child

Eighty years ago an Italian named Guglielmo Marconi was experimenting with his new invention, wireless telegraphy. In South Africa a 26-year-old firebrand, Winston Churchill, was "searching in the carelessness of youth for every scrap of adventure" as a reporter of the war against the Boers. The Prince of Wales was 59 and stout, Queen Victoria was 81 and failing. The sun was still shining on the great British Empire—but it was past midday.

In the summer of that same year, 1900, in a warm, brick Queen Anne house near Stevenage in Hertfordshire, now a stark town, but then a pretty village, Lord and Lady Glamis were expecting an addition to their already large family of five sons and two daughters—another daughter had died from diphtheria at 11. The eldest boy, Patrick, heir to the earldom, was 15; the youngest, Michael Claude, who was inclined to asthma, was six.

Lord Glamis, heir to the 13th Earl of Strathmore, was a Scottish aristocrat, proud of a family ancestry dating back to Robert the Bruce, King of Scotland. The Glamis were of royal blood, but they were not royalty, and nothing can have been further from their minds than that their youngest daughter, now to be born, would one day be Queen Consort and the last Empress of India—a country which, incidentally, Queen Elizabeth the Queen Mother has never visited.

Elizabeth Angela Marguerite Bowes-Lyon—the Lady Elizabeth Glamis—was born at the family's country house, St. Paul's Walden Bury, on Saturday, August 4, 1900. The start of a long life at the birth of the 20th century.

Her mother, Nina Cecilia, was the ▶

Above right: *An early portrait of the charming Lady Elizabeth Bowes-Lyon, aged five*
Above: *The comfortably-furnished Red Room at St. Paul's Walden Bury, sometimes called the Garden Room*
Right: *St. Paul's Walden Bury, only 30 miles from London, is one of the family homes of the Strathmore family*

daughter of the Reverend Charles William Cavendish-Bentinck, a cousin of the sixth Duke of Portland. Her father, who became the 14th Earl of Strathmore four years after Elizabeth was born, was descended from a long line of great Scottish families. In the 14th century King Robert II gave his daughter Jean's husband the title Lord Lyon and, as a dowry, the hunting lodge of Glamis. Seventy years later their grandson was created the first Lord Glamis in 1445. In 1540 a Lady Glamis—hated by James V—was burnt alive as a witch on Castle Hill in Edinburgh.

The 11th Lord Glamis and third Earl of Kinghorne was made the first Earl of Strathmore by King Charles II, but was hampered somewhat by a debt of £400,000, which he gradually reduced "by prudence and frugality".

It was not until the middle of the 18th century that the Strathmores found real wealth and, as with many well-connected families, it came about through marriage.

When George Bowes, a rich industrialist from County Durham, learned that the ninth Earl of Strathmore wished to marry his daughter Eleanor he raised no objection. Indeed he let it be known he was quite prepared to give over his entire fortune and all his estates in the North and in Hertfordshire—in his daughter's name naturally—provided the Lyon family change their surname to Bowes. The proud Lyons apparently agreed without demur. The marriage took place. And after the old magnate died they smartly changed their name once more, to Bowes-Lyon.

Lady Elizabeth Bowes-Lyon's father was a reserved, courteous and religious man with a prominent nose and bushy moustache. As Lord Lieutenant of Forfar, now Angus, he carried out his duties with great good conscience. He was an excellent shot, a better than average cricketer, (unusual for a Scot), and his knowledge of forestry was renowned. He was, above all, a kindly man.

But it was probably his wife who had the most lasting influence on their youngest daughter. The Countess of Strathmore was straight-backed and straight-principled. She embroidered beautifully and was so accomplished musically that she could attend a concert, return home, go straight to the piano, and play the pieces from memory. She had an intense zest for living, a lively sense of humour, an incapability of expressing herself without using her hands, and an open-door friendliness which often meant that young people especially would unburden themselves to her when they daren't utter a word to their parents. "Life is for living and working at," she would say, adding as admonition: "If you find anything or anybody a bore, the fault is in yourself."

She didn't believe in punishing children, but in setting an example. With her youngest daughter it was only necessary to say "Elizabeth", when she was naughty, and the child would hang her head in shame. In a moment, though, the fault and ▶

Above: *Two favourite pictures from the Strathmore family album of two-year-old Elizabeth at St. Paul's Walden Bury*
Right: *A gentle, always cheerful child—a miniature of Elizabeth at five years old*

Top: *Nine-year-old Elizabeth on her favourite Shetland pony, Bobs, in the grounds of St. Paul's Walden Bury*
Left, above and right: *Dressing-up was a favourite pastime and here Elizabeth and her younger brother, David, don fancy dress for an afternoon's entertainment*

the admonition were forgotten and Lady Elizabeth was back to being her friendly, cheerful self.

However, there was such a gap between Elizabeth and her next elder brother—some seven years—that it was fortunate that there came along a younger brother, David, born two years after her.

David and Elizabeth were inseparable. Their mother used to call them "my two Benjamins". Whether it was at St. Paul's Walden Bury, 30 miles from London, or at Glamis Castle, near Dundee, they found plenty to occupy and little to trouble their halcyon life before World War I.

On dry days in Hertfordshire there was Bobs the Shetland pony to ride, bullfinches to tame, chickens to feed, long lawns to race across, and a tumbledown brew-house to hide in. The nursery was the schoolroom— for doing sums on scratchy slates, and on wet days for reading full stretch on the floor in front of built-up fire and high brass fender.

Most of Lady Elizabeth's childhood was spent at St. Paul's Walden Bury, described by The Times in 1937 as "a comely house, much grown upon by magnolia and honeysuckle". Built in the early 18th century, it stands serenely among acres of peaceful English countryside that mainly the combustion engine has torn apart, with roads and noise and mechanised industry. Not far away, at Hatfield, Elizabeth I began her Tudor reign.

When she was in her twenties, Lady Elizabeth was to write a story about the everyday life of a little girl that bore a strong resemblance to her own childhood: ▶

Opposite: *The "two Benjamins"— Elizabeth with her beloved brother, David*

Top: *A painting of the Strathmore family in the drawing room at Glamis Castle*
Above: *The Scottish ancestral home— Glamis Castle—seen from the south*
Left: *Elizabeth at seven years old—the fringe would give way to a more modern style, but the pearls would remain as a kind of hallmark*

"At the bottom of the garden is the *wood*—the haunt of fairies, with its anemones and ponds, and moss-grown statues. . . . Whenever—and this is often—a dead bird is found in this enchanted wood it is often given solemn burial in a small box lined with rose-leaves.

"Now it is time to go haymaking, which means getting very hot in a delicious smell. Very often she gets up wonderfully early—about six o'clock—to feed her chickens and make sure they are safe. The hens stubbornly insist on laying their eggs in a place called the *flea house*, where she and her brother go and hide from Nurse. . . ."

St. Paul's Walden Bury was for winter, spring, and early summer. A tablet in the local church records that a Queen was born, baptised, and worshipped here. But in high summer or early autumn the family moved

Above: *Lord and Lady Strathmore with their children at St. Paul's Walden Bury. Back row, from left to right—Fergus, John, the 14th Earl of Strathmore, Mary, Patrick, Alexander; front row, from left to right—Rose, Lady Strathmore with David on her lap, Elizabeth and Michael*
Far left: *Elizabeth would share her love of dogs with her future husband*
Left: *The ancient granary and other outbuildings at St. Paul's Walden Bury were cherished haunts of childhood*

Above: *An early picture of the Duke of York, almost hidden behind Elizabeth, at a Strathmore family gathering*
Right: *Elizabeth, with her eldest brother, Patrick, Lord Glamis, and her father, Lord Strathmore, just before her wedding*

430 miles north, to Glamis, the castle in the Great Glen.

For children, and for adults, Glamis had all the history, the ghosts and the imagined battles to make the blood race.

Up the tower run spiralling steps, 143 in all, each cut from a single stone and so wide five men with swords can climb abreast. Shakespeare, the legend says, set the scene of Duncan's death at the hand of Macbeth inside the castle. Mary Queen of Scots lingered here and embroidered covers for a chair. Bonnie Prince Charlie, the Young Pretender, left a watch beside his bed in hasty escape from English soldiers.

A favourite game of the younger Strathmore children was to "repel raiders", that is to say, harmless visitors arriving in their Sunday best, by pouring boiling oil, that is to say, water, from the turreted roof. A favourite game that was not oft repeated.

Elizabeth, apart from one unhappy term, didn't go away to school, though her younger brother, David, did. Her mother taught her to read and write. Governesses came and went. The Lady Elizabeth, they reported, was a lively girl with an aptitude ▶

for languages—French especially—and a neat toe for dancing. She was nearly always cheerful—"a good wee soul to have about the place"—and quite able, even at nine years old, to entertain guests to tea if her mother happened to be detained.

After her mother, the greatest adult influence was undoubtedly Clara Knight, who came as a nurse, stayed on as a nanny and actually returned to care for Lady Elizabeth's first child, the Princess Elizabeth. She was known as "Alah"—the nearest the small children could get to pronouncing Clara. The daughter of a Hertfordshire farmer, she entered the service of the Strathmore family when she was 17, and only left when she died, at Sandringham, in 1946. At the funeral the Queen Mother, then the Queen, said to Clara's sister: "She mothered us all."

Only the very old, and those who know their history, will immediately connect the birthday of the Queen Mother with another altogether terrible event.

On August 4, 1914, the Lady Elizabeth was staying at her parents' London house in St. James's Square, and had been promised as a birthday treat a family visit to the vaudeville at the Coliseum. On the way the streets around Piccadilly and Trafalgar Square were chock-a-block with revellers waving Union Jacks. At midnight, back in bed, the young girl may just have heard the distant cheering of crowds pressing towards the railings of Buckingham Palace—patriotic fervour for a war that was going to cost millions of lives, among them that of her brother Fergus, killed in 1915 at the battle of Loos.

For the duration of World War I—the one that was "to be over by Christmas" but lasted four years—Glamis Castle was turned into a convalescent hospital for the wounded. Lady Strathmore and her youngest daughter became hostesses to a continuous stream of shattered, hobbling men, dressed either in khaki or the ill-fitting bright blue suits, white shirts and red ties that displayed to any carping doubters that they were not draft-dodgers but soldiers of the King.

Whenever a new batch of wounded arrived Lady Strathmore and her daughter were at the door to greet them, or toured the rooms soon after to give a comforting word. To some the visitation of a Countess and a Lady may have seemed almost an irrelevancy, but as they gazed out of a window their spirits were lightened by the sight of a pretty girl trying to bicycle with her eyes shut, by the same girl offering to write letters home for the disabled, or pop down to the village for a packet of Goldflake.

These men were the first to experience the natural warmth and friendliness that the Queen Mother has since shown to millions of other total strangers over the years. As a nervous hostess later remarked, when arranging an important dinner party: "Oh do let's ask Elizabeth Bowes-Lyon. She's so good at putting *everybody* at ease."

But at Glamis during World War I the Strathmore's youngest daughter was still

Above: *Elizabeth with her father in 1921*
Left: *As a lovely girl of 17*

Opposite—Above: *Elizabeth, with her sister, Lady Rose Leveson-Gower, shaking hands with a soldier who had convalesced at Glamis Castle during World War I*
Below: *Long country walks with the family have always been one of the Queen Mother's favourite pastimes*

only a teenager and the sight of maimed and disfigured bodies impressed her with an abhorrence that was never completely to leave her. To this day the Queen Mother has little sympathy for those who cosset themselves with trifling ailments.

A great deal of her time during the War was taken up with crimping tissue paper to fill sleeping bags, and even more with knitting socks and sewing shirts for the local battalion, the 5th Black Watch. One incident that has been remembered down the years is the fire which badly damaged some of the fine paintings and tapestries in the castle. It is remembered especially for the cool head which the young Lady Elizabeth showed in preventing a real catastrophe.

It was a Saturday evening and most of the soldiers had gone into Forfar to see a Charlie Chaplin film. The 16-year-old Elizabeth was walking in the castle grounds, even though it was December, when she spotted smoke coming from one of the windows of the central tower, some 100 feet up.

Lady Elizabeth ran inside and telephoned the Dundee fire brigade, 12 miles away. But before they arrived the castle could burn down. Far from being daunted, our heroine enlisted her young brother's help, and organised the servants and the few able-bodied soldiers who hadn't gone to the pictures. "The Dundee fire brigade will be here soon," she announced in a clear, piping voice. "I have telephoned them and the local brigade. Until they come we must form a chain of buckets and keep the fire at bay."

To a man, they obeyed their young commander's orders, so that by the time the fire brigade came racing up the causeway, bells a-clanging, the flames had been checked.

The reporter from the Dundee Courier and Advertiser, who arrived a little later, was most impressed. His long report includes the admiring line: "Lady Elizabeth Bowes-Lyon was a veritable heroine in the salvage work she performed, even within the fire zone."

But life was not entirely hard work and devotion to the needs of others. There was also the occasional dance and parties in London with officers back from the Western Front who needed cheering up.

Lady Elizabeth was 18 and extremely attractive when the war finally ended. She wore a fringe, pearls—nearly always pearls—and her spontaneous smile and often mischievous eyes made certain she was never short of admirers.

She loved going to parties and staying up late. Her brother David did not. Admittedly he was only 16, but even later this was to remain one of the few areas where their tastes differed. And after all, dancing and flirting did not take up all that much time. The favourite hours, as in childhood, were still those she spent in the open air, away from stuffy towns.

(Eventually Sir David was to marry Rachel Spender-Clay and to have two ▶

children. His death at only 59 in 1961 came as a crushing blow to his sister Elizabeth.)

In 1921 there were battles in Dublin, riots in Egypt; the King opened the first Parliament in Northern Ireland, and 85 million working days were lost in Britain through strikes.

And while, no doubt, Lady Elizabeth Bowes-Lyon read of these happenings in The Times, or in the Dundee Courier when she was at Glamis, there were other more romantic events taking precedence in her own personal life.

In September of the previous year her parents had organised a dance at Glamis Castle and among the guests they had invited was the second son of the King, the 24-year-old Prince Bertie, Duke of York, who happened to be staying at the time with neighbours, Lord and Lady Airlie.

A few months later Queen Mary, Prince Bertie's mother, confided to her friend Lady Airlie that she had discovered her son "is very much attracted to Lady Elizabeth Bowes-Lyon. He's always talking about her." Lady Airlie nodded, smiled and informed the Queen she had known the Strathmore girl all her life "and could say nothing but good of her."

Right: *The Countess of Strathmore with her youngest daughter at Glamis Castle*
Below: *Ready for an afternoon spin. From left to right—Lady Doris Gordon Lennox, Lord Settrington, Lady Elizabeth, the Hon. Bruce Ogilvy, the Earl of Haddington, Miss Alex Cavendish (seated) and the Hon. Diamond Hardinge*
Below right: *At the age of 21*

Love and marriage

Prince Albert, the future George VI, first met Lady Elizabeth Bowes-Lyon when she was five, at a children's party. He became an instant admirer, but several years would pass before they met again

Almost from birth the Duke of York had lived in the shadow of his elder brother, David, the dashing and immensely popular Prince of Wales. As children, both sons lived at times in near terror of their disciplinarian father, George V, and their mother, Queen Mary, was somehow never able to give them the tender love that children need.

The pockets of their sailor suits were sewn up so they couldn't put their hands in them. A sporran slightly askew on a kilt would bring a sharp reprimand from their father.

David tried, but failed most of the time, to please his father, though his charm and sudden enthusiasms quickly won others to him. Bertie, on the other hand, was much quieter and more shy. He was not rebellious, like his brother was. But he suffered from bouts of sulkiness and had a fierce, though short-lived temper, which was often directed at himself when he felt he had failed in some way.

As a child doctors recommended he wore splints for part of the day to straighten his knock-kneed legs. He was forced to write with his right hand when he was naturally left-handed, and by the time he was eight he had developed a stammer which he had to struggle for years to overcome and which drove him in on himself even further.

Meeting and falling in love with Lady Elizabeth Bowes-Lyon was, as he often told friends, the most fortunate thing that ever happened to him.

They first met at a children's party when, it is said, the five-year-old Lady Elizabeth gave him the crystallised cherries off her sugar cake. But they did not come to know

The happy couple take a break at a London tennis party, shortly after the announcement of their engagement in 1923

each other well until much later through Elizabeth's friendship with the Duke's sister, Princess Mary (they had a common interest in Girl Guide work) and Prince Bertie's meetings with one or other of Lady Elizabeth's brothers on the grouse moor.

By now Prince Bertie was in his twenties and more self-confident than he had been as a young boy. He had followed his father into the Royal Navy and undergone the harsh life of the midshipman in those days, training at Osborne and Dartmouth. He enjoyed naval life and stood up well to the

discipline. His ambition was to rise to the rank of captain, as his father had done, even though he hardly ever went to sea without suffering the nausea of sickness.

He saw action at the Battle of Jutland in 1916, and rose to the dizzy heights of acting Lieutenant, but after nearly four years of service, sickness forced him to leave the sea.

At his own suggestion, however, he took to the air—this, remember, was less than 10 years after Louis Blériot had been the first man to fly across the English Channel. Prince Bertie was not enamoured of flying, but he was determined to prove that he could become a pilot. And this he did, in 1919. The first member of the Royal Family to gain his "wings".

Prince Bertie was not especially good-looking—not as dashingly handsome as his elder brother—but he had a certain shy charm, which ladies found was a pleasant alternative to the sweaty exuberance of the Hooray-Henries. The men he mixed with liked him because, apart from anything else, he was not at all a bad shot!

Compared with the dry protocol of Court life and the stiff relationships within his own family, the King's son found the Strathmore's family life excitingly different. Everyone seemed genuinely to like everyone else. There was a warmth, a complete lack of stuffiness, and an unforced spirit of gaiety among them. Being "family" was almost more important than anything else to the Strathmores.

"It is delightful here," he wrote from Glamis to Queen Mary, "and Elizabeth is very kind to me. The more I see of her the more I like her."

The Duke of York (as he had now ▶

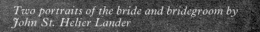

*Two portraits of the bride and bridegroom by
John St. Helier Lander*

become) courted Lady Elizabeth with quiet determination for nearly two years. For her part, though she was supremely happy in Bertie's company, the thought of marriage, of moving from the informal country life she had known since childhood into the public glare and perpetual round of royal duties, was something that needed thinking about. Rumours have persisted down the years that the Duke proposed no less than three times before being accepted. But when a reporter at the time dared to ask for confirmation, he received only the cryptic response: "Do you think I am the sort of person Bertie would have to ask twice?"

Certainly the King was not entirely confident of his son's chances of winning Lady Elizabeth, the girl voted the best dancer in London. "You'll be a lucky fellow if she accepts you," he chuckled. At the same time both he and the Queen were quite sure that Elizabeth was the one woman who could make their son happy. The fact that it was very rare for a Royal Duke to marry a commoner did not concern them too much. Their eldest son, who would one day be King, would himself almost certainly marry a suitable person soon and produce an heir of his own. There would be no problem, they thought.

On a Saturday in January 1923, strolling through the bare woods of her home in

Top: *On the moors at Glamis in August 1923. Elizabeth, the Duchess of York, walks beside the Prince of Wales*
Above: *On a visit to Edinburgh before their marriage*
Left: *Lady Elizabeth leaving her parents' home in Bruton Street for the Abbey*
Opposite—Above: *The family wedding group*
Right: *The crowd give the Royal couple a rousing send-off on their honeymoon*
Far right: *Their first home— White Lodge in Richmond Park*

Hertfordshire, Lady Elizabeth Bowes-Lyon, 22, accepted the marriage proposal of His Royal Highness Prince Albert Frederick Arthur George, Duke of York, 27.

As soon as he got back to the house the ecstatic Duke sent off a telegram to Sandringham with the pre-arranged signal: "All right. Bertie." Two days later he formally told his parents of the engagement. "We are delighted, and he looks beaming," wrote Queen Mary in her diary.

One of Lady Elizabeth's married sisters, Lady Rose Leveson-Gower, stated to a reporter of the day: "Her intimate friends regard her as of the best type of girlhood, with a healthy taste for outdoor life in the countryside, and a keen enjoyment of the amenities of society in town. Lady Elizabeth is not only a good sportswoman . . . but she is clever with her needle and a lover of the arts that go to the making of a happy home."

The date fixed for the wedding was April 26; the place, Westminster Abbey. It would be the first time in over 500 years that a Prince of the Royal House had been married there. The last was King Richard II in 1382.

To record such an important historic occasion and bring it to the people, the BBC asked for permission to place microphones discreetly round the Abbey. However, the ▶

application was unfortunately turned down.

In chilly weather the bride left the Strathmore's London home, now moved to Bruton Street, Mayfair, in a State landau, escorted only by four mounted policemen, and because she was not yet "royal" the troops lining the route to Westminster Abbey did not present arms.

However the crowds gave their own spontaneous salute, with cheers for a bonnie Scottish bride they had already taken to their hearts.

The wedding dress, of simple medieval style with a square neckline, was made of fine chiffon moiré, embroidered with silver thread and pearls. The train was of old point de Flandres lace, lent by Queen Mary, with underneath a longer train of Nottingham lace. This lace, incidentally, was specially chosen to help boost ailing home sales—imports of Continental lace had thrown thousands out of work in the Nottingham area.

Included in the bride's trousseau was a white garden party dress, a tennis dress of apple-green cotton edged with periwinkle blue silk, many tea-gowns, several Quaker cloche bonnet-shaped hats, "of which Lady Elizabeth is so fond", a full-length sable squirrel coat and an evening wrap of white lapin with roses of fur let into the skirt.

A woman's page editor at the time wrote: "The Bride's dresses are of the lightest and flimsiest materials and are of great beauty but no splendour."

Five Indian princes and a score of European kings and queens, princes and princesses came to London for the wedding. Searchlights were trained on Selfridges, there was dancing in four ballrooms at the Savoy. For the wedding breakfast an eight-course banquet was served in the State Dining Room of Buckingham Palace. The wedding cake, nine feet high, weighed a staggering 800 pounds.

The marriage ceremony itself was touchingly simple by comparison. By order of the King there were no flowers decorating the Abbey lest they detract from the plain dignity of the pillars, but on the Tomb of the Unknown Warrior, throughout the service, lay the bride's bouquet of white York roses, placed there spontaneously by Lady Elizabeth as she entered the church, a last act of remembrance before she became the Duchess of York.

An ordinary suburban train with a rather extraordinary carriage attached took the newly-weds from Waterloo on the first

Above left: *The Duke and Duchess of York on their wedding day, April 26, 1923*
Far left: *Though shooting was his first love, the Duke of York thoroughly enjoyed hunting, too*
Left: *Enjoying a stroll during their honeymoon at Polesden Lacey*

stage of their honeymoon. The extra carriage was upholstered in gold brocade and overwhelmed with white roses, carnations and lily of the valley. It took them as far as Bookham, on the way to Dorking. From there they motored to Polesden Lacey, an early 19th-century house, lent by a friend, Mrs. Ronald Greville, which is now a National Trust attraction.

A fortnight later they travelled north to Glamis to spend the rest of their honeymoon in biting wind, rain and snow. The Duchess was confined to bed for much of the time, with whooping cough. "Not a very *romantic* disease," the Duke afterwards commented. They returned south to their first home—White Lodge in Richmond Park.

King George V wrote to his son from Balmoral a few weeks later: "The better I know and the more I see of your dear little wife, the more charming I think she is, and everyone feels in love with her here."

A writer in The Times commented: "Whilst the Princes of Wales have almost invariably been compelled to accept the brides that State policy selected, the Dukes of York have nearly always obeyed the dictates of their hearts."

Right: *Called The Red Carnation, this portrait was taken just before Elizabeth's marriage*
Below: *Arriving for a stay at Glamis in 1925*

Above right: *One of the rare photographs of the Duchess of York in uniform—on this occasion as Vice President of the Girl Guides*
Right: *Happy days at Southwold, at one of the Duke's annual camps for boys from public schools and industry*
Far right: *Besides shooting and hunting, the Duke was a keen golfer*

Queen Mary

Top: *King George V, Queen Mary and Queen Alexandra head the procession to watch the great Victory Parade of 1919*
Above left: *Queen Mary, when Duchess of York, with her three eldest children— Edward, Albert and Mary (centre)*
Above right: *Queen Mary celebrates the opening of Bedford College's new home in Regent's Park in July 1913*
Left: *Queen Mary with her new daughter-in-law at Balmoral in 1923*
Right: *A picture that epitomises the public image of Queen Mary—formidable but kind*

Top left: *Shaded by a giant parasol, Queen Mary tours the British Empire Exhibition at Wembley in April 1924*
Top centre: *As the Princess of Wales shortly before the death of Edward VII*
Top right: *With her second son, Albert (Bertie), at the age of two*
Above: *Only a few years before he became King, the Prince and Princess of Wales on holiday with their children at their Scottish home, Abergeldie, near Balmoral*

To those meeting her for the first time or even seeing her only at a distance, Queen Mary was a most formidable lady. She will go down in history as one of the last of the traditionally regal figures, above the people and remote from them.

As a prospective mother-in-law she could be expected to make any girl tremble. And yet the reputation was probably more forbidding than the reality. The young Duchess of York had great respect for Queen Mary, but she was certainly not afraid of her. The gap between them was that of a generation and totally different upbringings.

Princess May of Teck had a sense of duty running through her like a rod of steel. As a young woman she had been chosen to marry the Duke of Clarence, eldest son of the future Edward VII, and as he was dying of pneumonia a few months after their engagement had heard him call out the name of the woman he had really wanted to marry.

In duty, and in love, the Princess went on to marry Prince Eddy's younger brother, George, and in time became his Queen.

All her life Queen Mary was basically shy, solemn, and almost incapable of unbending. Even when she was dining alone with the King she wore full evening dress with tiara, and the King wore tails. "It seems to me," she remarked as early as 1914, "that 'finesse' has gone out of the world, that indescribable something which was born in one and which was inherited through generations."

"She remained tragically inhibited with her children," wrote her close friend Lady Airlie. "She loved them and was proud of them but ... they were strangers to her emotionally."

For her part Queen Mary was immediately attracted to Elizabeth. She was not at all flighty like so many "gals" at the time. She had obviously been brought up in a loving family, but one with *principles*. She marvelled at Elizabeth's seemingly natural ability to bring warmth and light-heartedness to any occasion, without losing dignity. She could draw people out, something Queen Mary had never been able to do. The Queen was so glad that Prince Bertie had found a girl who could make him happy.

The King, who could be decidedly crusty at times, was overjoyed by the young woman's gaiety. He could forgive her anything, even being late. To arrive for a 12 o'clock appointment when the clock was chiming the 11th stroke was to be unpunctual, in the King's eyes. So when his son and daughter-in-law arrived apologetically two minutes late for dinner one evening, everyone waited for the ticking-off. Instead the King smiled. "You are not late, my dear," he said. "I think we must have sat down two minutes early."

Some well-meant kindnesses were not so easy to accept. When the Duke and Duchess of York returned from their honeymoon it was arranged by Queen Mary for them to set up their first home at the White Lodge in Richmond Park, where the Queen had grown up and her eldest son had been born.

It was a fine house, but it badly needed modernising. While the young couple were still on their honeymoon, the Queen thought it a good idea to busy herself with furnishing the place with some of her own exquisite antiques, though she did nothing about the plumbing.

The bride returned to a house and furniture that was perhaps not quite what she would have wished for her first home, but she did not complain. She knew the effort, and love, that had gone into the preparations for her.

When, a few weeks later, the Duke and Duchess entertained the King and Queen to luncheon for the first time in their new home (the Duke had written to his mother warning that "our cook is not very good"), Queen Mary returned to the Palace and wrote that she thought they had made their home "very nice".

Lilibet and Margaret Rose

A Press statement released on April 21, 1926 officially announced: "Her Royal Highness the Duchess of York was safely delivered of a Princess at 2.40 this morning. Both mother and daughter are doing well."

The newspapers reported the birth, but made little of it. The country was in industrial turmoil. Over a million were out of work; there was bitterness, resentment and gnawing hunger. In the minds of many the birth of a pretty princess in a fine London house called for no special rejoicing. Thirteen days later the country was to be crippled by the General Strike, which lasted nine days.

It had not been an easy birth, but at least it took place in the Duchess's parents' comfortable home in Bruton Street and not in the less familiar surroundings of White Lodge.

Present, by long tradition, was the Home Secretary of the day. The practice dated back to the time of James II when, it was alleged, there had been an attempt to switch babies in a warming pan. The custom, which he thought unseemly and archaic, was finally ended by the Duke when he became George VI and his elder daughter was expecting her first child—Prince Charles.

King George and Queen Mary were woken shortly after 3 a.m. with news of the arrival of their first granddaughter, and later that day a small crowd gave them a cheer as they arrived from Windsor for their first glimpse of "a little darling with a lovely complexion and pretty fair hair."

The baby was named Elizabeth Alexandra Mary, and christened by the Archbishop of York in the private chapel at Buckingham Palace.

"You don't know what a tremendous joy it is to Elizabeth and me to have our own little girl," the Duke wrote to his mother.

Much to their consternation, when their

Above: *A charming portrait by John St. Helier Lander of the Duchess of York with her first child, Princess Elizabeth. Although the little Princess was in direct line of succession, no-one foresaw the events that would lead to her being crowned as Queen 27 years later*
Far left: *The Duchess of York leaving Bruton Street for her daughter's christening at Buckingham Palace on May 29, 1926*
Left: *A happy family reunion after their first Royal tour in 1927. King George V and Queen Mary are on the left and the Earl and Countess of Strathmore on the right*

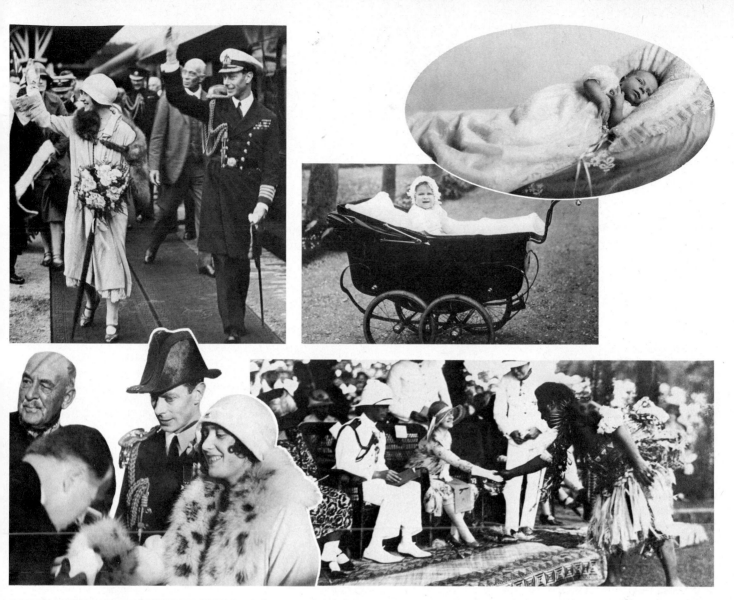

Top left: *The tour of 1927 was an outstanding success and greatly increased the Duke of York's self-confidence. Here the Royal couple wave farewell to the crowd at Maitland, New South Wales, Australia*
Top right: *Two pictures of the little Princess—three weeks old and as a one-year-old in her pram*
Centre left: *At Las Palmas, their first port of call on the Royal tour*
Centre right: *A meeting of different cultures at Suva, capital of Fiji*
Above: *During the tour, the Duke managed to fit in some deep-sea fishing in the Bay of Islands, New Zealand*

baby was only a few weeks old the King informed the Duke and Duchess that they would be going to Australia and New Zealand the following year on an official tour that would mean an absence from home, and their baby daughter, of six months.

Even the Australians were none too pleased by the news. They had been hoping that the Prince of Wales would be coming to open the Parliament in their new federal capital of Canberra. He had been to Australia and New Zealand in 1920 and had set the people's hearts alight. The Duke of York, on the other hand, was an almost unknown quantity.

The tour was to be the Duke and Duchess of York's first major assignment together, and they both knew the greatest threat to its success was the Duke's terror of making public speeches.

In easy conversation with friends he hardly stammered at all, but with strangers or on platforms the struggle to speak certain words was painful to watch.

The Duke had tried any number of remedies, all to no avail. "The disillusionment caused by the failures of previous specialists to effect a cure," wrote his official biographer, Sir John Wheeler-Bennett, "had begun to breed within him the

inconsolable despair of the chronic stammerer and the secret dread that the hidden root of the affliction lay in the mind rather than in the body."

In 1926 the Duke was recommended to an Australian speech therapist, living in London, and the treatment this time really seemed to give hope. It called for hard work and much patience over a long period, involving a new method of breathing. And as the therapist, Lionel Logue, emphasised, it was vital that the Duke had the support and encouragement of his wife.

Over a period of months the Duke and Duchess religiously worked away together, the Duchess listening daily to her husband reading aloud and patiently coaxing him to do his exercises. There was noticeable improvement.

On January 6, 1927 the Duke and Duchess left Portsmouth in the Renown— the battle cruiser that was to end her days on the ocean floor, sunk by a Japanese air attack in 1941.

The Duchess was desolate at leaving behind their baby, even though she knew she would be well cared for by nannie Clara Knight, the faithful friend who had been with the family since before the Duchess's own birth. She went back twice to kiss ▶

Elizabeth after she had placed her in the nurse's arms in the hallway at Bruton Street. On the way to the railway station the chauffeur was asked to circle Grosvenor Gardens more than once, so that his lady passenger could recover her composure before facing the official farewells and the crowds at Victoria.

Throughout the tour coded cables were dispatched each week giving the Duke and Duchess up-to-the-minute news of their daughter. Every month Marcus Adams, the celebrated photographer, took pictures of the Princess so that they would miss as little as possible of their daughter's progress.

The King reported that the Princess had four teeth, "which is quite good at 11 months old," and the Duke wrote back saying he hoped she wasn't being spoilt by her grandfather.

The voyage of the Renown covered 30,000 miles and took the royal visitors by way of the Panama Canal to the Marquesas Islands, Fiji, New Zealand and Australia. As expected, they were welcomed everywhere by enthusiastic crowds, but the Duke found it hard to believe the people were cheering him as well as the Duchess. It was plain to everyone how popular she was. The smile, the little wave, the way she listened with utmost concern when anyone spoke of a personal problem or tragedy— "she shines and warms like sunlight", wrote an ardent Scot.

When his wife was taken ill with tonsillitis and forced to leave the tour for a while, the Duke seriously considered cancelling his engagements too. He was not sure he could carry on without her at his side.

Those thousands who watched him make speech after speech, struggling to get the words out, saw also how the Duchess sat on the platform looking straight ahead, undismayed, but sharing every painful moment with him, and giving him such strong silent support.

The general consensus at the end of the tour was that while the Prince of Wales had been immensely popular on his tour of 1920, the Duke of York had been liked better. And the Duchess was a sensation!

Princess Elizabeth was eight-and-a-half months old when her parents left home, over 14 months old and on the point of walking when they returned.

While they had been away, arrangements had been made for the family to move into 145 Piccadilly, which has since been demolished. Again Queen Mary looked after the refurbishing in their absence.

The four-storey house at Hyde Park Corner, rented on a yearly basis, was to be the Yorks' home for the next nine years. On the Duchess's instructions, it was decorated in her own favourite pastel shades, with chintz covers on many of the chairs and settees. At the entrance to the morning room were positioned the two tusks of the elephant shot by the Duke in Uganda in 1925. A fire escape was installed, leading from the nursery floor to the small back garden.

For the next three years the Duke and

Top left: *By the time the tour had reached Wellington, the people had warmed to the Yorks. Here the Duchess inspects the Wolf Cubs in Wellington, New Zealand*
Top right: *Before they passed through the Panama Canal, the Duke and Duchess of York spent three days in Jamaica*
Above: *Playing deck tennis on board HMS Renown*
Below: *After a highly successful tour, the Duke and Duchess of York come ashore at Portsmouth on June 27, 1927*

Duchess led a blissful existence together. They often dined out in public, and went dancing at a favourite nightclub.

They also took a serious interest in improving housing and working conditions of the less privileged. Employers and trade union leaders were regular callers at 145 Piccadilly to discuss how industrial relations could be improved. The Duke's famous annual Boys' Camps, started in 1921, brought public schoolboys and young factory workers together. In all these efforts to improve society and at the same time provide a more useful role for royalty, the Duchess gave her husband invaluable support.

"No-one knows better than I do," the Duke told an audience in Glasgow, "how great is the help which she has given me in my public duties."

On Thursday, August 21, 1930, a day of rain storms and lightning, the Duchess of York gave birth to her second daughter. This time the event took place at Glamis Castle, and in celebration—the Princess was the first member of the Royal Family to be born in Scotland since 1602—the Glamis pipe band, in full regalia, led the villagers to the summit of Hunter's Hill, two miles distant, and there they lit a beacon and drank two large barrels of beer.

The Duke and Duchess had planned to name the baby Ann—"Ann of York sounds pretty"—but when they discovered King George did not care for the name at all, they decided on Margaret Rose, which satisfied everyone.

The four-year-old Princess Elizabeth, who was called Lilibet because that was how she pronounced her own name, thought ▶

Top right: *The young Princess Elizabeth on the way to the Trooping the Colour ceremony in 1933 with her mother and grandmother. Also in the carriage are the Princess Royal and her son, Viscount Lascelles*
Right: *Princess Margaret Rose was the first Royal child to be born in Scotland for over 400 years*
Below left: *An admirer of little Princess Margaret looks on at a Balmoral fête*
Below right: *One-year-old Margaret poses for a portrait with her mother and sister*
Far right: *The two Princesses outside the play-house at Royal Lodge, Windsor*

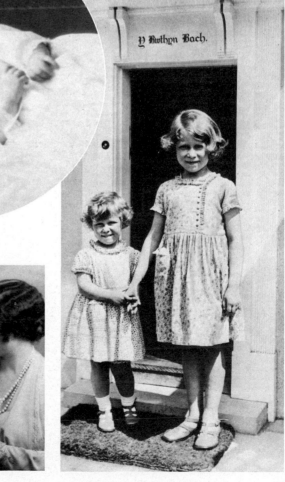

her sister should be called "Bud", because she was too small to be a rose.

Following the King's attack of pleuro-pneumonia in 1928, from which he nearly died, Princess Elizabeth started the practice of going to a front window of 145 Piccadilly after breakfast and waving good-morning and good-health to her grandfather in Buckingham Palace just across the park. And very often the King was there to wave back. For weeks it was a regular habit. The old King adored both his granddaughters, Elizabeth perhaps a little more because she was the first and, like him, quite serious about most things. Margaret Rose was always the demonstrative one.

Each morning the Princesses were taken to see their parents, and at lunch they were allowed into the dining room during dessert. Whenever official duties permitted the Duchess would slip upstairs to join them in the nursery, and again in the evenings at bath-time. When they were old enough she taught them both to read, and with their father played a succession of parlour and card games. It was a much more affectionate and homely life than he had ever known as a child. It was as much like her own happy childhood as the Duchess could make it.

Both parents would have liked their eldest child to attend school, but the King would not hear of it. In those days, children in close succession to the Throne did not have that sort of close contact with other children.

So "Crawfie", the governess, took them through their curriculum—a course of studies criticised by Queen Mary at one point for not paying enough attention to history and Bible reading. There were dancing lessons and piano lessons, and occasionally "instructional tours" of London's landmarks with Queen Mary.

The Duchess introduced her children to the tricky business of how to address certain people by playing the part of an archbishop,

Top: *A charming study of a Royal mother with her two children*
Left: *Sandringham, in Norfolk, where the young Princess Elizabeth stayed with her grandparents when the Duke and Duchess of York were in Australia*
Above: *Playing in the sand at St. Paul's Walden Bury*

a prime minister, or a president and asking the Princesses to guess who she was supposed to be, and tell her the correct form of address.

Most afternoons, except in the worst weather, a horse-drawn carriage would draw up outside the house and the two Princesses would be taken for a ride round Hyde Park or Battersea Park. Everyone soon came to know about it, and the children received far more affectionate exposure to the public than royal children are permitted by their parents today.

Countless admirers had pictures of the two little Princesses pinned up in their homes, and children were forever sending them gifts. Their popularity became so great—passengers on the top deck of buses could look down into the back garden of 145—that the Duke and Duchess began looking for somewhere more private outside London where they could escape at weekends.

The choice fell on Royal Lodge, then called *The* Royal Lodge at the King's insistence, in Windsor Great Park. The house, once occupied by the Prince Regent, was in a bad state of repair. The gardens ▶

Right: *Arriving at Olympia for the Royal Tournament in 1935*
Below: *With one of their favourite dogs at Royal Lodge, Windsor*
Far right, above: *A compulsory breath of fresh air with nanny, Clara Knight*
Far right, below: *Fun and games at Abergeldie Castle fête in 1933*

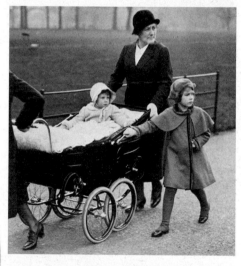

were a tangle of rhododendrons and briar. It took a year to make the place habitable, but the work, on the garden especially, gave the Duke and Duchess, and their children, great family pleasure.

The Princesses were given their own little garden to cultivate, and an aviary for their blue budgerigars. The first of the long line of Royal corgis was introduced— Rozavel Golden Eagle, more commonly known as "Dookie".

Queen Mary had never allowed dogs in Buckingham Palace, but the Duchess of York had grown up with dogs around her and she thought it important her children should benefit from their company too.

These were supremely happy years for the whole York family. The rumbling threats of war from across the Channel still seemed fairly distant. Much nearer home, a crisis endangering the Throne itself was not even being considered.

Occasionally at weekends the Duke of York's elder brother would drop in at Royal Lodge to inspect the improvements his brother and sister-in-law had made. The Prince of Wales was particularly interested in the work done on the landscaping because he had tackled the same problems with the ground surrounding the grace-and-favour house he occupied only a few miles away. Sadly, Fort Belvedere was never to know the lasting happiness of Royal Lodge, the Queen Mother's favourite home to this day.

Above right: *A Royal trio, taken by the celebrated photographer, Marcus Adams, in 1934*
Right: *The whole family together, in 1936, at the Princesses' play-house at Royal Lodge, Windsor*
Below: *Smartly dressed for an outing to an official function*

An artist's impression of the last hours of lying-in-state of King George V, showing the King's four sons keeping vigil

Death and abdication

The words of the last medical bulletin on King George V, broadcast over the radio, unintentionally but perfectly described the end of an era: "The King's life is moving peacefully to its close." Events of the next two years were to shake the very foundations of the monarchy, some feared irreparably, and the lives of the Duke and Duchess of York, and of their children, were never to be the same again.

"I miss him dreadfully," the Duchess wrote to the King's doctor after George V's death in January 1936. "Unlike his own children I was never afraid of him, and in all his 12 years of having me as a daughter-in-law he never spoke one unkind or abrupt word to me, and was always ready to listen and give advice on one's own silly little affairs. He was so kind and so *dependable*."

The same could not be said, unfortunately, of his successor Edward VIII. The four sons of the dead King, who stood in motionless vigil at the lying-in-state of their father in Westminster Hall, were so different in character, one from the other.

Edward—David to the family—was boyish, charming, highly personable and feckless. Henry, Duke of Gloucester, was stolid, military, country-loving. George,

Duke of Kent, was funloving and impressionable, the one son who even as a child instinctively knew how to humour his father. And Bertie, Duke of York, demonstrating each year more and more of the same characteristics as the old King. Steadfast, excessively punctilious, a navy man, uneasy in the company of intellectuals. In fact, a person not so very different from millions of other subjects of the new King, which is partly why people liked the Duke of York.

Edward was someone who dazzled them. Daring in the saddle, a jaunty figure with a cigarette in the corner of his mouth and a twinkle in his eye, he seemed to go on being young when everyone else was growing old—a feat to be envied and mistrusted at the same time.

He was 41 when he came to the Throne, but no-one thought of him as being middle-aged. Everyone had such high hopes at the beginning—well, nearly everyone. Clement Attlee, leader of the Opposition told Parliament: "As Prince of Wales he endeared himself to all hearts. He is continuing in a higher sphere and with greater responsibilities the work which he has been doing so well for this country."

Even the Tory Prime Minister, Stanley

Baldwin, who was to be faced with a constitutional crisis as a result of the King's actions only a few months later, said on his accession: ". . . he has the secret of youth in the prime of age; he has a wider and more intimate knowledge of all classes of his subjects, not only at home, but throughout the Dominions and India, than any of his predecessors . . . We look forward with confidence and assurance to the new reign. . . ."

Perhaps they were fooling themselves, or fooling the people. Or simply unaware of what was going on. For at that time only a few people knew of the existence, let alone the influence, of Mrs. Wallis Simpson. King George V did, and he is supposed to have confided in Mr. Baldwin in the autumn before his death: "After I am gone, the boy will ruin himself in 12 months." And to have told the Countess of Airlie, a close family friend: "I pray to God that my eldest son will never marry and have children, and that nothing will come between Bertie and Lilibet and the Throne."

The Duke of York had always been fond of his elder brother. The close alliance between them dated from early childhood and a shared dread of their father's sharp ▶

chidings. In later life King George grew to love and respect Bertie, but to the end David nearly always disappointed his father, however hard he tried to please. His behaviour was the antithesis of staidness, and both King George and Queen Mary were nothing if not staid.

The people found his rebelliousness, and his quite genuine desire to influence an improvement in the lot of the common man a refreshing change from the aloof stance usually adopted by those in his privileged position. Most of them, and certainly most women, even approved of his dallying with one woman after another. It was all part and parcel of being the dashing Prince of Wales. Somehow, nothing was quite so simple—for Prince or people—when Edward became King.

When she married, the Duchess of York was aware how close her husband and his brother were. But from early on it became apparent that, though she had some liking and sympathy for him as a person, the Prince of Wales' world was not her world. It never had been. Before her marriage she had gone out with several men and she had certainly enjoyed dining and dancing, and kicking up her heels.

But that was only a phase, a natural phase in any young woman's life. A happy marriage and home life had always held higher priority. To the Prince of Wales brittle talk, supercilious women, spur-of-the-moment adventures and needless extravagant gestures seemed to be the way of life he either couldn't escape from or had no desire to relinquish. He had been so eager to race away from the restrictions imposed on him in youth he appeared now incapable of slowing down to maturity.

And yet there were signs that, with the right woman, he might settle. He was as happy as his brother when together they were tackling down-to-earth tasks like clearing overgrown gardens and watching bonfires take. He enjoyed being in a warm family atmosphere. The York children, Princess Elizabeth and Princess Margaret Rose, always made him feel welcome at

Royal Lodge. Uncle David was such *fun*.

But after he became King the whole family saw less and less of him. The friendly intimacy became increasingly strained. Of course, as King, the burdens he had to carry were onerous. And he set about them with characteristic enthusiasm—to start with. But perhaps he began to lose interest when he fully appreciated that it was the Government that was ruling the country, and not he, and that his advice was by no means always welcomed or taken. At any rate, highly confidential Cabinet papers went unread for days. Some traditional public appearances were carried out unwillingly, and long-standing customs were thrown out overnight, for no immediately obvious good reason.

In the summer of 1936 the King chartered a yacht and sailed round the Dalmatian coast and the Greek Islands with a party of friends that included Mrs. Wallis Simpson. Photographs wired to the world's Press showed that a good time was being had by all. But with incredible restraint, the British Press made no reference to any

Above left: *The two eldest brothers accompanying their father's coffin on the journey from Sandringham to London*
Above: *The funeral procession slowly makes its way down Piccadilly*
Below: *David and Bertie had always had a close relationship, but this would not survive the abdication crisis*

close connection between the King and the American divorcee from Baltimore.

The Duke and Duchess of York, however, were aware of the rumours that were being headlined in Continental and American newspapers. If the relationship continued, or more especially, if David insisted on marrying Mrs. Simpson, then they feared the final outcome. There could be no suggestion, in their minds, of a King marrying a divorced woman and remaining King. As the Duchess pointedly told Winston Churchill when he made reference at a dinner party to the scandal of King George IV and Mrs. Fitzherbert: "That was a long time ago."

Precisely on how many occasions the Duchess met Mrs. Simpson in the months leading to the abdication is not on public record. And the Queen Mother has reserved her opinions of the woman for very nearly half a century. It is a subject she would still rather not discuss, even with her most intimate friends.

However, the Duchess of Windsor (as she became after her marriage to David) tells in her memoirs of an occasion early in 1936 when the King and she drove to Royal Lodge in order to show off a new American station-wagon he had just bought. The Duke was not at first particularly impressed, but allowed himself to be taken for a spin, and evidently changed his mind about the car. After they returned the Duke and Duchess, the King and Mrs. Simpson went for a stroll in the gardens.

The King's future wife thought rather highly of the young Duchess: "I had seen the Duchess of York before on several occasions at the Fort and York House. Her justly famous charm was highly evident. I was also aware of the beauty of her complexion and the almost startling blueness of her eyes."

Tea was taken in the drawing room. Princess Elizabeth, then 10, and her five-year-old sister joined the party. Most of the talking evidently took place between King Edward and the Duchess of York.

The Duchess of Windsor's memoirs continue: "It was a pleasant hour, but I left with a distinct impression that while the Duke of York was sold on the American station-wagon, the Duchess was not sold on David's other interest."

The whole Royal Family hoped the King's feelings for Mrs. Simpson were an infatuation that would pass, just as his love for other women in the past had faded.

At Balmoral, the favourite place where by tradition the whole family came together each autumn, the Duchess of York behaved impeccably when Mrs. Simpson appeared on the guest list. The overpowering chic of the lady and her somewhat misplaced proprietorial attitude towards servants was chauvinistically forgiven by other guests as being merely what one might expect from an American.

For a long time the British people were kept totally ignorant of the fact that their King had fallen hopelessly in love with a twice-divorced woman—Mrs. Simpson ▶

Top: *The Prince of Wales, before he became King, with other members of the Royal Family at Epsom on Derby Day*
Above: *King Edward VIII with Mrs. Wallis Simpson. Their relationship led to a constitutional crisis*
Right: *The Duchess of York with her brother-in-law, the Prince of Wales, who enjoyed the warm and friendly atmosphere of the York family*

Top left: *The British Press breaks its silence and the debate on the King's future becomes public*
Top right: *The public were sharply divided on the abdication issue and converged on Downing Street*
Above left: *The Prime Minister, Stanley Baldwin, felt the British people would never*

accept a Queen Wallis
Above: *King Edward VIII—a king who was never crowned*
Right, above and below: *The Press barons who supported the King. From left to right (above)—Lord Northcliffe, Esmond Harmsworth and his father, Lord Rothermere; (below) Lord Beaverbrook*

was granted a decree nisi on her second marriage at Ipswich on October 27, 1936.

When they did learn of what was going on—a sermon by the Bishop of Bradford, Dr. Walter Blunt, finally unleashed Fleet Street's constraint—shock was followed by fierce debate in just about every home in the land. "Let him marry who he wants, poor fella." "He's the King! Duty comes first, love must come second." "She can't be Queen of England! She's American!" "It'll do the monarchy good if he marries her. Bring it into the 20th century." "If he's allowed to marry that woman, the British Royal Family will be finished, we'll be a republic within 10 years."

The King had three choices. He could defy his ministers, marry the woman he loved and bring about a monumental crisis. There could be, possibly, a morganatic marriage, whereby she would be his wife, but not his Queen, and their children would have no position in the line of succession. Or he could renounce her. Towards the end Mrs. Simpson did in fact leave the country at her own suggestion, to await the final

decision of the King and his ministers.

But the debate in the country was on a more emotional level. The division was essentially between those who were for the King personally, as a human being with a terribly difficult decision to make, and those who saw his behaviour as a threat to the very institution of monarchy, conceivably leading to civil war. The matter must be handled delicately, but very firmly.

Supporting "the King's case", as it was called, were the powerful Press barons Beaverbrook and Harmsworth, and the volatile Winston Churchill. In a much more difficult position, simply because he was Prime Minister, was Stanley Baldwin. Conservative by nature, and one suspects not a romantic, Baldwin could not see any course open to the King, if he persisted, other than abdication. The Church of England would not allow a King to marry a divorcee, and the country as a whole, Baldwin believed, would finally make up its mind that, however much they sympathised, the King must go.

For several weeks Edward VIII fought a

defiant battle with his ministers and with his conscience. He wished to keep the Throne, but he would not, could not, give up the woman he loved: "I cannot with full heart carry out my duties in the loneliness that surrounds me."

After months of trying to find another way out, he took the irrevocable decision. "I want you to be the first to know," he told Baldwin. "I have made up my mind and nothing will alter it. I mean to abdicate and marry Mrs. Simpson."

Almost two years later Queen Mary was to write to her son: "You did not seem able to take in any point of view but your own . . . It seemed inconceivable to those who had made such sacrifices during the war that you, as their King, refused a lesser sacrifice . . . My feelings for you as your Mother remain the same, and our being parted and the cause of it, grieve me beyond words. After all, all my life I have put my Country before everything else, and I simply cannot change now."

The Duke of York was equally shocked by his brother's decision to abdicate, but

David was not surprised that "Bertie was so taken aback by my news that in his shy way he could not bring himself to express his innermost feelings at the time." For, as he wrote in his memoirs: "next to myself Bertie had most at stake: it was he who would have to wear the crown if I left, and his genuine concern for me was mixed up with the dread of having to assume the responsibilities of kingship."

Both the Duke and Duchess of York went through an agony of waiting during the first week of December 1936. They did not know whether the King had definitely decided to abdicate, and yet the Prime Minister apparently did. The Duke telephoned his brother several times, asking for news, but was put off each time. He was kept waiting four days for the summons, to be told that the reins were now in his hands.

Though there is no official record open to the public, there are some grounds for the suggestion that the delay may have been due to consideration being given, for a short time at least, to the Crown passing to the Duke of York's younger brother, the Duke

of Kent, who already had a son. It may have been thought that the burden of kingship might prove too much for the Duke of York and his daughter who would follow him. If so, events have proved the doubters were mistaken on both counts.

In the final days of the crisis, the Duchess of York, who had given such unfaltering support to her husband all along, was forced to her bed with a bad attack of influenza.

Shortly after she was informed of the King's decision, her children's governess, Marion Crawford, entered the bedroom and the Duchess, propped up by pillows, held out a hand to her. "I am afraid there are going to be great changes in our life, Crawfie," she said, ". . . we must take what is coming to us, and make the best of it."

On his last evening in England before sailing to France in a naval destroyer, King Edward VIII finished his radio broadcast to the nation with these words: "And now we all have a new King. I wish him, and you, his people, happiness and prosperity with all my heart. God bless you all. God Save the King."

Top left: *The ex-King says farewell in a radio broadcast from Windsor*
Top right: *The day of abdication*
Above left: *The marriage of the Duke and Duchess of Windsor took place in France on June 3, 1937*
Above: *The first public royal recognition of the Duchess of Windsor took place in 1967, at a ceremony to unveil a plaque to Queen Mary. Here, the Queen Mother talks to the Duke of Windsor*

From house to palace

On the first night of his reign King George VI demonstrated to Lord Louis Mountbatten exactly how he felt. "I never wanted this to happen. I'm quite unprepared for it . . . I've never even seen a State paper. I'm only a naval officer, it's the only thing I know about."

Lord Louis calmed his kinsman's fears by, typically, telling a story of how George V came to Mountbatten's father in similar distress when he was about to become King. "My father answered: 'There is no more fitting preparation for a King than to have been trained in the Navy'." He might have added: "and to have a good wife."

Many people close to the King believed he could not have done the job he was now committed to without the support of a gentle but strong woman. Bertie had never liked the limelight. He felt awkward and inadequate whenever it fell on him. Whereas Elizabeth, who was not naturally a show-off, seemed to glow in its warm beam. In a New Year's message to the Empire and the Commonwealth, the King said he realised to the full the responsibilities of his "noble heritage" and shouldered them "with all the more confidence in the knowledge that the Queen and my mother Queen Mary are at my side."

Like her husband, the Queen had been stunned by the abdication and the thought of how it would affect all their lives. The family had been happy at 145 Piccadilly and at Royal Lodge at weekends. Now, suddenly, they were moving to the huge rooms and endless corridors of Buckingham Palace. When told, 10-year-old Princess Elizabeth exclaimed with horror: "Not for ever?", and suggested the only way to make such a move palatable was to build an underground passage all the way from the Palace to the beloved Royal Lodge at Windsor.

Immediately the Queen went about giving a more homely look to the private apartments at the Palace. Her kidney-shaped dressing-table, and her four-poster bed were moved from 145 Piccadilly. Plans were made for the wallpaper to be changed to something lighter, and in a very few weeks she had the place looking a good deal less stuffy.

At the same time arrangements were going ahead for the solemn act of crowning. Coronation Day was to be May 12, 1937—the date that had already been set aside for King Edward VIII's coronation. This gave less time than usual for preparation, but the new King was anxious to have a happy public occasion as soon as possible after the disruption of the abdication.

However, the haste, along with a decision to postpone a visit to India, contributed to a flurry of gossip in London that the King was a sick man. He was an epileptic. He had a weak heart. The length of the Coronation service was being shortened because of his health. There were even rumours that the

Above left: *The Queen arriving at 145 Piccadilly, which had been the family home for over nine years*
Above right: *One of the first formal portraits of the Queen, by Cecil Beaton, photographed at Buckingham Palace*

Left: *The crowning of Queen Elizabeth as Queen Consort—a rite going back to Saxon times. And in the oval inset, the crowning of her husband, King George VI*
Below: *Many of the people lining the procession route had camped out all night to secure a good view*
Bottom left: *The newly-crowned King and Queen pass through Trafalgar Square in the State Coach on the slow journey back to Buckingham Palace*
Bottom right: *The Royal Princesses precede their parents through Trafalgar Square*

Coronation would be cancelled altogether!

The newspapers, as usual, drew attention to the stories simply by denying them. In their hearts many people still believed that the King was perhaps mentally ill, and that while he would continue to reign he would seldom appear in public and would be purely "a rubber stamp" for government decisions.

No-one can be sure who or what started the rumours—the King was in fact in excellent health at the time. Fortunately, helped by a speech he made without hesitation on April 23, the slanders disappeared before Coronation Day.

Like his father, the King was a deeply religious man, of simple faith, who attached great importance to the vows he was about to take in Westminster Abbey.

On the Sunday evening before the Coronation he and the Queen returned to Buckingham Palace after a quiet weekend at Royal Lodge for a meeting with the Archbishop of Canterbury, Dr. Cosmo Lang. It was timed to take place during the hour when, in churches throughout the country, prayers were being offered for Their Majesties. Dr. Lang spoke of the spiritual aspects of the Coronation, and then, he recorded, the King and Queen knelt down with him, "and I gave them my personal blessing. I was much moved, and so were they. Indeed, there were tears in their eyes when we rose from our knees. From that moment I knew what would be in their minds and hearts when they came to their anointing and crowning."

Before then, however, there was not much sleep to be had! In the notes he made on the same night, the King described how his Coronation Day began at 3 a.m. when he and the Queen were woken up by loudspeakers being tested outside their bedroom windows. At five o'clock massed bands and columns of soldiers, with their attendant sergeant-majors, paraded up and down in rehearsal, "so sleep was impossible. I could eat no breakfast and had a sinking feeling inside. I knew that I was to spend a most trying day and to go through the most important ceremony of my life."

For several days beforehand the Queen rehearsed with her husband the responses he would have to make—his voice would be heard by millions on the radio—and together they went through the order of the service time and again.

Queen Elizabeth insisted that precedent should be broken so that Queen Mary could see her son crowned—the widow of a King was not supposed to witness the coronation of his successor. This in turn meant that Queen Mary would after all require her crown, which had already been passed on to her successor. Accordingly another had hastily to be made for Queen Elizabeth.

The Queen's purple robe was a combined ▶

A selection of commemorative souvenirs of the 1937 Coronation. The plate, mug and embossed tins are familiar Royal souvenirs. But the busts (one rather gaudy), figurine and jigsaw are rather more unusual

Left: *During the build-up to the Coronation, the streets of London took on a festive air and everywhere people demonstrated their loyalty to the new King and Queen*
Inset: *"No Entry" says the sign, but two sightseers have shinned up the pole for a better view*

Above: *The King reviews his Fleet at Spithead in 1937—one of the traditional celebrations that follow a Coronation*

cape and train, embroidered with the emblems of the 10 countries of the Empire, and lined and edged with ermine. Princess Elizabeth and Princess Margaret Rose were dressed in purple velvet with ermine capes and lightweight gilt circles.

On May 12 it rained, as it nearly always does on important royal occasions, but nothing deterred the thousands who had slept the night before on the soggy grass of Green Park and Hyde Park. They were going to have their Coronation procession after all, not for the King they expected to see crowned (the Duke and Duchess of Windsor's activities were still occupying columns of newsprint), but for his brother who they were beginning to respect much more.

The crowds lining the route were 20 deep in some places. A grandstand seat outside the Abbey sold easily for 25 guineas. Most people listened to commentary on the radio, but perhaps a few thousand watched the BBC's first ever "live" television coverage—from outside the Abbey; there was never any question of television cameras being allowed *inside*.

Despite all the pre-planning and split-second timing the elaborate proceedings of the Coronation did not pass without mishap. A Presbyterian minister fainted when the procession down the centre aisle was about to begin and there was evidently "no place to which he could be taken," wrote the King. "I was kept waiting, it seemed for hours, due to this accident."

The Dean of Westminster very nearly placed a surplice inside-out over the King's shoulders. When the moment came to read the Coronation Oath the Archbishop of Canterbury's thumb covered some of the words. The tag of red cotton, indicating the front of the St. Edward's Crown, was not there when it came to the actual moment of crowning. And as the King prepared to move majestically from the Coronation Chair to the Throne he realised one of the bishops was standing on his robe: "I had to tell him to get off it pretty sharply as I nearly fell down."

The Queen fared better. There were no mishaps. She was crowned Queen Consort, in accordance with a practice going back to Saxon days, and thereby stood in rank above Queen Mary and Princess Elizabeth, the heiress presumptive.

"Then the Archbishop shall take the Crown from off the Altar into his hands, and reverently set it upon the Queen's head, saying: 'Receive the Crown of glory, honour and joy'."

That evening the King and Queen appeared five times on the balcony of Buckingham Palace to acknowledge the cheering of the crowds, and a chain of beacon fires stretched the length of the country.

In the summer months that followed there was a Naval Review at Spithead, a state visit to Scotland, and a service of thanksgiving at St. Paul's Cathedral in London. With every public appearance the King seemed more sure of himself. He detected with some surprise that people's affection was directed towards him as well as towards the Queen.

Up till now Bertie had depended to a great extent on the support of his wife. It was she, it appeared to observers, who took the lead, who instinctively knew how to approach total strangers and put them at their ease. But from now on a change in the relationship was noticeable. It was as if, now that he was actually King, the taciturn Bertie had finally found confidence in himself and was able to give support to his wife. The Royal couple became a loving partnership, each depending on the other. No-one was happier than the Queen to see how things were developing. She was so proud of her husband, and the way he had measured up to his awesome responsibilities. She so agreed, in this matter at least, with the King's elder brother who on his abdication had prophesied: "You'll make a good king, Bertie."

Family album

The Royal Family must face more photographers and see more photos of themselves than any other family in the world. But this hasn't put some of them off taking their own family snaps. One member of the Royal Family—the Duke of Kent—is an extremely proficient and talented amateur portrait photographer.

Prince Charles and his younger brother, Prince Andrew, have never shown a lasting interest in recording events for family posterity, perhaps because they have grown used to their mother clicking the shutter at them on so many occasions.

The Queen Mother has taken many family photos in her time, but she probably prefers turning the pages of family albums of photos that others have taken. When she was a young girl cameras, except the ever popular box-Brownie, were complicated to operate. Nowadays they present few problems, but are still somehow frightening. She is someone who, on the whole, would rather that *you* took the picture.

Top inset: *Queen Elizabeth with her daughters in 1941*
Top: *The King and Queen enjoying a picnic on the Scottish moors in 1949*
Centre insets: *The two Princesses help out in the garden at Windsor*
Above left: *In Portsmouth, for the review of the Fleet in 1937*
Above right: *A family group round the hearth at Buckingham Palace in 1942*

Top left: *The Princesses in their pony cart at Windsor Castle, their wartime home*
Top right: *Planting a tree at a friend's birthday party in Scotland, 1937*
Centre left: *As Duke and Duchess of York, on a visit to Skye in the early 1930s*
Centre right: *The Royal Family join in the singing at the King's Camp at Abergeldie in Scotland, 1939, only a few weeks before the outbreak of World War II*
Above left: *The Duke of York taking part in the men's doubles championship at Wimbledon in 1926*
Inset: *Queen Elizabeth with her eldest daughter at Royal Lodge, Windsor, in 1946*
Right: *The Royal Family at Windsor in 1946. A year later, Princess Elizabeth would marry Prince Philip*

Children will be children

The constant exposure to the public eye of the Royal Family demands considerable qualities of its members—composure, restraint and, not least, the ability to stand still! But as these pictures show—children will be children.

1. At a Scottish fête in 1933
2. Leaving St. Paul's Cathedral after the Silver Jubilee service of King George V and Queen Mary in 1935
3. Introductions at the ceremony to plant a Coronation oak at Windsor in 1937
4. Princess Elizabeth salutes the guard of honour at the Royal Tournament in 1931
5. Summer 1939 at the King's Camp at Abergeldie, near Balmoral
6. The Queen Mother with her granddaughter, Princess Anne, watching the Trooping the Colour in 1959
7. Three-year-old Princess Elizabeth takes a rest at an official function
8. Out for a ride with Queen Mary

A portrait of the Queen Mother, at 37, as Colonel-in-Chief of the King's Own Yorkshire Light Infantry by the late Sir Oswald Birley

To the New World

American President Franklin D. Roosevelt's characteristically warm personal invitation—"Do come and visit us, and bring the children with you"—heralded the first ever visit of a reigning British Sovereign and his Queen Consort to the United States.

The King wanted to accept the invitation very much—it followed on another, made at the time of the Coronation, to visit Canada. The plans were to combine the two into an official tour.

However, the early summer of 1939 did not seem the most propitious time to leave behind the shores of England. Hitler had contemptuously torn up the Munich Agreement—"peace in our time"—after less than seven months, and marched into Czechoslovakia. Mussolini was puffing up his peacock pride at the expense of lives in Abyssinia and Albania. There was a deep sense of foreboding in Europe—the dictators were drumming and the din was growing closer.

In the event, the King and Queen decided to make the trip across the Atlantic, but in a liner instead of a battle-cruiser as planned—it might be needed in a hurry elsewhere—and the two Princesses were considered too young to go.

The Arctic ice-floes had come much further south than usual that year and the Empress of Australia's passengers spent an eerie four days in dense fog among the icebergs, with memories of the Titanic disaster in 1912 only too near. The melancholy blasts of the ship's siren "were echoed back by the icebergs like the twang of a piece of wire," wrote the Queen. When eventually they came into view, the sight of cheering crowds on the quayside at Quebec was heartwarming.

The people of Canada gave the King and Queen a tumultuous reception—something not altogether expected because although George VI was King of Canada, there had been talk of secession from the Commonwealth and of neutrality if Britain ever had to go to war. But even French-speaking Canadians now talked about "our King and Queen."

The Queen, as usual winning the hearts of everyone—especially the Scots

Above left: *On board the Empress of Australia at the start of the tour*
Inset: *The Queen smiles at the crowds gathered to welcome the Royal visitors to Canada*
Far left: *The King and Queen leave the Canadian Parliament in Ottawa*
Left above: *Thousands turned out to glimpse their Majesties as they drove through Montreal in an open car*
Left below: *On the last stage of their Canadian tour, the King and Queen visited a hospital for war veterans in Edmonton, Alberta*

Canadians—with her homely ways, watched with pride and pleasure the way the King grew in confidence. He was immensely touched by the warmth of the people's reaction to his presence: "I nearly cried at the end of my last speech in Canada, everyone around me was crying." Both were to remark several times on how the tour of Canada "has made us".

Altogether the King and Queen travelled over 4,000 miles by Canadian National Railways, greeted along the route by thousands who had also travelled long distances from prairie farms and settlements for a brief glimpse of the royal visitors. At Unity, Saskatchewan, population 680, the crowd grew to 20,000. Often the train had to slow down in normally wild deserted country, so that the King and Queen could wave to families along the track. Once, when they had got out to stretch their legs, the King—wearing shorts—came across two Russian émigrés who dropped to their knees in astonishment and awe.

As the route brought them near to the American border, the roads were jammed with thousands of sightseers driving out from Detroit. Of the Queen, the Governor-General of Canada, Lord Tweedsmuir, remarked: "She has a perfect genius for the right kind of publicity."

The King and Queen's reception over the border in the United States was just as enthusiastic. "In the course of a long life I have seen many important events in Washington," wrote Mrs. Roosevelt, the President's wife, in her diary, "but never have I seen such a crowd as lined the whole route between the Union Station and the White House. They have a way of making friends, these young people."

Most Americans had never seen a king. They thought he would be stand-offish, and he wasn't. He was highly amused by the Senator who grasped his hand on Capitol Hill, glanced at the woman at his side and said: "My, you're a great Queen-picker."

The Queen was concerned at the disappointment of a little girl who thought Their Majesties were not dressed like the kings and queens in her story books. So she arranged for the eight-year-old child to be in the hall of the White House later the same day as she and the King left for dinner at the British Embassy—he wearing the Order of the Garter insignia, and she a regal picture in crinoline, jewels and diadem. "Oh Daddy, oh Daddy," the little girl cried, "I have seen the Fairy Queen!"

An American columnist nominated the Queen "Woman of the Year". "Arriving in an aloof and critical country, she completely conquered it and accomplished this conquest by being her natural self."

Exhausted but exhilarated, the Royal couple returned to Canada before leaving for home after a month of dinners, speeches and brilliant public relations work. The Queen, in a radio broadcast, told the Canadian people: "This wonderful tour of ours has given me memories that the passage of time will never dim. . . ."

Top: *The King chats with President Roosevelt on the drive from Union Station to the White House in Washington DC*
Above: *Relaxing on the porch of the Roosevelt's private home in Hyde Park, on the Hudson River. From left to right—Mrs. Franklin D. Roosevelt, King George VI, Mrs Sarah Roosevelt (the President's mother), Queen Elizabeth and President Roosevelt*
Left: *The Queen examines a medal worn by a Girl Scout after a Girl Scouts Parade in Washington*

Queen and country

In early September 1939, on a Sunday morning at 11, Prime Minister Neville Chamberlain spoke to the British people over the radio, and the whole world listened. He told them that the time was up. The Germans had ignored the ultimatum and given no undertaking to withdraw their troops from Poland: ". . . consequently this country is at war with Germany."

Like most parents with young children, the King and Queen had hurriedly to make arrangements. Many people had seen the war coming, but everyone had hoped it wouldn't happen. So very little preparation had been made.

Princess Elizabeth, 13, and Margaret Rose, who was nine, were already at Balmoral. It was decided, for the present, that they should remain there. Queen Mary, now in her seventies, went to Sandringham, and then on to Badminton, the Duke of Beaufort's estate, where, as a contribution to the war effort, she spent some time laying claim to any scrap metal she saw lying around the countryside. Once or twice the "scrap" turned out to be perfectly usable farm equipment, which had to be quietly returned to its owner.

At Buckingham Palace the staff was depleted through men being called up for active service and families being evacuated to Windsor. The horses that pulled the state coaches were sent to Windsor, to work on the farm. Display cases were emptied of their priceless ornaments and turned to the wall so that, in an attack, shattered glass could not fly out and cause injury.

In the parks, trenches and vast underground air-raid shelters were being hurriedly excavated. The shelter at the Palace was a converted housekeeper's room in the basement, with a reinforced ceiling and steel shutters at the window. Axes were supplied, for emergency escape, but the furniture somewhat incongruously comprised gilt chairs, a regency settee, and round table. There was also a bottle of smelling salts and a pile of Country Life and Sphere magazines.

During the first few months—called "the phoney war" because everyone had expected instant aerial bombardment, and none came—the King and Queen toured defence posts and docks, and praised the families in the small towns and villages who had manfully coped with a sudden invasion

Top inset: War was officially declared on September 3, 1939
Top: Refugees from many of Europe's Royal Houses were welcomed at

Buckingham Palace. Among them were Queen Wilhelmina of the Netherlands, King Haakon of Norway; below, King Haakon's son, Crown Prince Olav and King Peter and

Queen Alexandra of Yugoslavia
Centre left: *Prime Minister, Neville Chamberlain, broadcasts the declaration of war to the nation*
Left: *Children in their thousands, clutching treasured possessions and gas-masks, were evacuated from the cities to the safety of the countryside*

of thousands of bewildered child evacuees from the cities.

In the spring of 1940 they made welcome their own class of refugees—monarchs from Europe whose countries had been overrun by the terrifyingly swift advance of the German armies.

The King went to Liverpool Street Station to meet Queen Wilhelmina of the Netherlands who had escaped across the Channel in a British destroyer. On the same day, by another route, came Princess Juliana, and her daughters Princess Beatrix, aged two, and the nine-month-old Princess Irene.

Only three weeks after the arrival of Queen Wilhelmina, the King again went to the station, Euston this time, to meet King Haakon of Norway and Crown Prince Olav, who had spent two months dodging the German invaders.

After Dunkirk and the fall of France, with the enemy poised only 20 miles away across the Channel, there was increasing concern for the safety of our Royal Family. There was every possibility that the Germans would attempt an airborne commando-type raid to capture at least one of them. A special squad of Guardsmen—called the Coates Mission after their commander, Colonel Coates—was formed specifically to protect the Royal Family. Their job was to get them away to one of four "safe" houses located far from London, should the Germans invade.

The King was supplied with a bulletproof car, and work was speeded up on a proper bomb- and gas-proof shelter at the Palace. He carried a Sten gun, hidden in a briefcase, and, like everyone else, never ventured outside without a gas-mask—the Queen preferred to carry hers in a dolly-bag rather than a bulky box, and though she was issued with a steel helmet she was never known to wear it.

A small target range was set up in the gardens of Buckingham Palace where the King and Queen, together with members of their staff, practised assiduously with pistols and tommy-guns. The Queen had lost none of the touch that she had shown on safari in Uganda 15 years before. Her aim was deadly accurate. So was the King's. Winston Churchill was so impressed he brought the King an American short-range carbine—"from a number which had been sent to me. This was a very good weapon."

Both he and the Queen were clearly able to defend themselves. But there remained the problem of how best to protect their two children. Princess Elizabeth and Princess Margaret were equally in constant danger of kidnap or being killed by a bomb.

The suggestion was made that they should be evacuated to Canada for the duration of the war. Many other parents, including young Princess Juliana of the ▶

Above right: *Royal visits to bomb-damaged areas did much to boost morale*
Right: *Their Majesties, accompanied by Winston Churchill, inspect bomb damage to Buckingham Palace*

Netherlands, had already taken that precaution. However the Queen would hear none of it. "The children won't go without me. I won't leave the King. And the King will never leave."

Officially it was announced that the Princesses were "residing in a house somewhere in the country." In fact they were living within the stout protective walls of Windsor Castle—along with the Crown Jewels which had been hurriedly placed, almost higgledy-piggledy in the vaults. There they stayed for most of the war, deprived like other wartime children of simple pleasures such as sweets, bananas and new toys, which were practically unobtainable.

As in the days before the war, the Princesses represented all that was "good" about "nice" children, so their propaganda value was not overlooked. In October 1940 Princess Elizabeth, only 14, made a radio broadcast that was heard throughout the Empire.

"I can truthfully say to you all that we children at home are full of cheerfulness and courage. We are trying to do all we can to help our gallant sailors, soldiers and airmen, and we are trying, too, to bear our own share of the danger and sadness of war. We know, every one of us, that in the end all will be well."

The Princess had been well rehearsed by her mother, and she spoke beautifully, but the moment that brought a tear to many an eye came at the end when she turned to her sister and said, in a very unrehearsed voice: "Come on, Margaret." There was a pause while the 10-year-old, sitting at her side, drew breath. "Good-night, children," was all she said, but it was enough. The broadcast was a grand morale booster.

In the autumn of 1940 the blitz began, and the Palace did not entirely escape the destruction. The first bomb, with a delayed-action fuse, lay outside the north wing for a day. When it went off it shattered the windows of the Royal Apartments, but fortunately no-one was injured.

Three days later the King and Queen returned from a weekend at Windsor with the children, in the middle of an air-raid. They were unable to use their usual sitting room because of the broken windows, so they sat in a small room overlooking the quadrangle until, in the King's own words: "all of a sudden we heard the zooming noise of a diving aircraft getting louder and louder, and then saw two bombs falling past the opposite side of Buckingham Palace into the quadrangle. We saw the flashes and heard the detonations as they burst about 80 yards away."

Altogether six bombs straddled the building. One wrecked the Chapel—the site is now occupied by the Queen's Gallery—and another landed in the garden.

The King evidently laughed about their lucky escape, and the Queen was quite calm. But even though Churchill inspected the damage with them later, he was completely unaware how near to death they had been until after the war, when he asked them for their memories for the history he was writing.

Nonplussed, but wiser, they took a glass

Top: *The Queen, with members of the Royal Household, contributing to the war effort*
Insets: *Princess Elizabeth and Princess Margaret remained at Windsor for the duration of the war*
Above left: *With her sister looking on, Princess Elizabeth rehearses her broadcast to children, given in 1940*
Above right: *The King and Queen at Buckingham Palace, the home they refused to leave—"We stay put with our people"*

of sherry, lunched with members of their Household in the air-raid shelter, then in the early afternoon, as planned, went to visit blitz victims in dockland. "I'm glad we've been bombed," the Queen said. "It makes me feel I can look the East End in the face."

Altogether the Palace was hit nine times during the war, on six occasions when the Queen was there. But in common with everyone else who reached 1945 with a house still standing and limbs intact, both she and the King counted themselves lucky compared with others.

The King had been reigning less than three years when the war broke out—not enough time many thought for confidence and respect in the monarchy to be restored. What sort of King would he be to his people in wartime? Could he, like his brother did at certain moments, inspire the country, or was he, as some suspected, too shy and nervous in crowds to be of much use? Was he physically strong enough to stand up to the strains of duty?

Before long the King was to satisfy all his critics, but there were some criticisms he could make too. For one, the choice of Winston Churchill, the extrovert who supported his brother in the abdication crisis, as Prime Minister. The King would have preferred Lord Halifax to take over from Neville Chamberlain.

But as the months passed the two men's respect and admiration of each other increased greatly. Churchill was particularly pleased when the King suggested that instead of the formal weekly audience, at around 5 p.m., that the King traditionally gave to his Prime Minister, Churchill should come to lunch every Tuesday to discuss how the war was going.

The practice continued for four-and-a-half years. "On several occasions we all had to take our plates and glasses in our hands and go down to the shelter to finish our meal," Churchill wrote. Long before the war's end the two men were firm friends.

In a way they epitomised some of the more admirable features of the British character. Churchill, the bulldog, the man who rants and raves, but gets things done. And the King, reserved, unassuming, yet also possessing his own, less noticeable, brand of courage.

None of this is to forget the presence, and the influence, on both men of the Queen. With his genius for choosing the right words Churchill summed it up thus: "Many an aching heart found some solace in her gracious smile."

The Prime Minister was referring to the effect of the Queen's visits to the wounded in hospital, and to those who had lost relatives in the blitz. But the spirits of both Churchill and the King, especially in the darkest days when there seemed so little hope of victory, were often lifted by the very presence of the Queen. As one Cockney bomb victim put it: "She came with courage in her eyes, and when she left, she left some of it with you. Suddenly you felt like carrying on, when you hadn't before."

Yet the Queen seemed almost totally ▶

Top: *The King and Queen talking to volunteer workers at a wartime agricultural camp*
Centre: *By 1941 Sandringham Park had been ploughed up and put under crops. Here the Royal Family tour the estate by pony-trap and bicycle during the harvest of 1943*
Above: *A formal photograph of the Royal Family during the war years*
Left: *The two Princesses on stage in one of the Christmas pantomimes that were put on at Windsor Castle*

unaware of the effect she had on those who met her. When Lord Woolton, the Minister of Food, put his plan to the Queen for vans to be rushed to the blitzed areas carrying hot food and drink, he asked permission to call them Queen's Messengers. And when the Queen asked why: "what will *I* have done?", Lord Woolton was surprised to find she didn't apparently know "what you mean to all of us.

"It isn't only your high position it's the fact that people think of you as a person who would speak the kindly word and, if it fell within your power, would take the cup of hot soup to the needy," he said. The words were perhaps slightly parsimonious, but the Queen was delighted to hear them none-the-less. "Do you think I mean *that*? It's what I've tried so hard to be."

It was what the Queen had been brought up to be. The lady from the big house whose responsibility it was to visit the sick and help the poor. Not very fashionable notions in our modern welfare state, but genuine individual thoughtfulness for others shines through any clogging blanket of bureaucracy. And it was this kind of caring that endeared so many to the Queen.

Whenever news arrived of heavy bombing on a particular town, plans were made for the King and Queen to tour the stricken areas within hours. And in the midst of chaos, personal tragedy and shock, nobody seemed to mind the sight of a spotlessly groomed official party picking its way over the rubble towards them.

In general, people were taken totally by surprise when the King and Queen dropped in—because of security there was seldom advance notice. As they toured the bombed streets the King would often lag a little behind his wife, gathering facts and figures on casualties from officials, while the Queen would ask individuals about personal escapes or tragedies. They were quite intrigued on one occasion in Cardiff to meet four men, one after the other, who reckoned their lives had been saved by hiding under the stairs. "I think half of Cardiff must have been under the stairs that night," said the King.

On another occasion, when she came across a woman weeping because her dog was trapped under fallen masonry, too frightened to come out, the Queen volunteered she knew something about dogs. She

Top left: *The Queen helping her daughters with their schoolwork in the grounds of Windsor Castle*
Centre: *The King and Queen visit an Air-Raid Precaution (ARP) centre in the early months of the war*
Inset: *On a visit to a London hospital, which had itself been recently bombed*
Far left: *Encouraging words for a soldier about to join the front line*
Left: *In 1945, 18-year-old Princess Elizabeth joined the ATS, the forerunner of the Women's Royal Army Corps*

went down on her knees and coaxed it to the surface.

Millions will always remember the example set by both the King and the Queen during the war. Not so often recalled are the personal tragedies suffered by them. In the summer of 1942, the King's youngest brother, the Duke of Kent, was killed when the aircraft carrying him to Iceland crashed in Scotland. He was only 39. His youngest child, Prince Michael, was only seven weeks old. Two years later the Queen's father died, only a few years after her mother had died in 1938. She was devoted to them both.

The Queen, along with so many thousands of others, was to know the agony of waiting for news of a loved one who has gone on a dangerous mission. When the King flew to North Africa in 1943 to visit his armies there—using the code name General Lyon—there was an unexpected "blackout" on his progress lasting some hours. "Of course I imagined every sort of horror," the Queen wrote in a letter to Queen Mary, "and walked up and down my room staring at the telephone."

As the war dragged on, life at Buckingham Palace did not escape the tedium of rationing and austerity. Mrs. Eleanor Roosevelt, wife of the American President, noted when she came to stay that her vast bedroom was heated by one small electric fire. Some of the baths in the Palace had a painted line nine inches above the plug-hole to mark the prescribed patriotic level.

Amazingly, meals were still served on gold and silver dishes, but "our bread was the same kind of war bread every other family had to eat. Except for game that occasionally appeared, nothing was served that was not served in any ordinary war canteen."

Five years is a long time out of any life and the years of war were to alter British society irrevocably. Children especially missed out on so much because of the war. "Poor darlings," King George wrote in his diary on the first day of peace, referring to his own children, "they have never had any fun yet."

Winston Churchill, the historian, spotlighted one outcome of the war that was so obvious it might have escaped notice. "This war," he wrote to the King, "has drawn the Throne and the people more closely together than was ever before recorded, and Your Majesties are more beloved by all classes and conditions than any of the princes of the past."

The King, in his broadcast to the nation on August 15, 1945 spoke with a hint of the prophet rather than the historian.

"The war is over. You know, I think, that those four words have for the Queen and myself the same significance, simple yet immense, that they have for you. Our hearts are full to overflowing, as are your own. Yet there is not one of us who has experienced this terrible war who does not realise that we shall feel its inevitable consequence long after we have all forgotten our rejoicings of today."

Top: *VE Day, May 8, 1945, and the Royal Family, with Winston Churchill between them, wave to the jubilant crowds from the balcony of Buckingham Palace*
Centre: *A time of national rejoicing. Celebrations like this one in Piccadilly Circus were repeated all over Britain*

Oval: *Decking the streets with bunting ready for a Royal victory tour*
Above left: *The Royal Family watch the great victory parade on June 8, 1946*
Above right: *Tired but happy Londoners at the end of a long night's celebrations*

Gardens of peace

Above left: *The Duke and Duchess of York with Princess Elizabeth in the grounds of Royal Lodge, Windsor. The gardens were laid out by the Duke and Duchess and much of the work was done by their own hands*
Above right: *As King and Queen, with Princess Margaret, at the Chelsea Flower Show in 1951*
Left: *The Queen Mother exploring the delights of a town garden in Paddington*
Right: *Cecil Beaton's birthday photograph of the Queen Mother, taken on the terrace of her favourite home, Royal Lodge, in 1970*
Below left: *The Royal Family in the rock garden at Royal Lodge*
Below right: *The King and Queen inspect the Princesses' personal plots at Royal Lodge. The pedestal was given to the Queen by Queen Mary*

I f there is peace to be had, it is surely to be found in a garden. These sentiments were shared equally by the King and Queen. Each had been introduced to gardening as children and, fortunately, the introduction had not put them off for life!

The Queen learned the rudiments from her mother, Lady Strathmore, who was recognised as being one of the outstanding gardeners of her day. The head gardener's cottage at Glamis glittered with a closely packed array of trophies won at shows.

The Queen's childhood garden at Glamis Castle was a plot measuring about six feet by 12 feet in which she was allowed to grow anything she liked. She chose, in fact, a red rose climbing up a rustic pole as a centre piece, polyanthus and grape hyacinths round the base, with a variety of scented thyme as an edging border.

The King's first garden was altogether more challenging—240 square yards at Frogmore, in Windsor Little Park, planted with Brussels sprouts and other vegetables. Gardeners did the heavy digging, but Prince Bertie, as he then was, did the sowing and was expected to keep the weeds down to a manageable level.

In essence, the King was later to become a landscape gardener, while the Queen's strength was to lie in the ability to plan a flower bed to the best effect. She has always loved flowers for their shape and their scent. Very often she will pick a rose or nip a bloom of honeysuckle as she walks slowly round a garden, breathe in its perfume, then pin it to her dress. The Queen was never the kind of gardener who is happiest on her hands and knees grubbing out weeds.

During World War II part of the gardens at Buckingham Palace were turned over to vegetables and it took a year or two to restore the flower beds and rose gardens to their former glory. The manure for these, incidentally, is bought in, while the manure from the Royal Mews, next door, is sent out to a market gardener. Apparently, the reason for this untypical lapse in good husbandry is lack of space near to the Palace to store large amounts of horse manure.

After the war the King and Queen spent as much time as possible at Royal Lodge, Windsor, where they had worked at the garden for nearly 20 years. "Now that really is my garden—I made it—go and see it," the King told the eminent horticulturist, Dr. Shewell-Cooper. His pride was the way he had cleared acres of wilderness to create truly magnificent vistas stretching into the distance.

Here, and at Balmoral, he and the Queen used often to sit on the terrace in the evenings, and with the eye of an artist the King would discuss a branch that should be lopped or a bush that should be planted to improve the view. He was an expert on rhododendrons and loved to plan walks winding away from the house between banks of subtly changing shades. The King's opinion was that all the royal gardens—at Buckingham Palace, Windsor, Balmoral, Sandringham—suited the individual houses they surrounded.

The Queen's view has always been closer to home. A hedge of lavender surrounds Royal Lodge and near at hand are the sweet peas, which she likes to grow in profusion and hardly stake at all. She likes discipline in a garden, but it should not be too obvious. Rigid lines of bamboo stakes are anathema ▶

to her. Roses should be pruned hardly at all.

Queen Elizabeth was to retain all her life the happiest memories of Birkhall, eight miles from Balmoral, with its three summer houses where Princess Elizabeth and Princess Margaret Rose as children used to take it in turn to invite their parents to tea. Birkhall, overlooking the river Muick, was where Princess Elizabeth and Prince Philip spent their honeymoon, and Prince Charles enjoyed many happy childhood days.

At Balmoral, to the right of the front door, is a climbing white rose called Bonnie Prince Charlie which, not surprisingly, is a family favourite. Incidentally, you will not find any ericas planted at Balmoral. The King and Queen thought that with heather in glorious profusion on the surrounding hills, there was good reason not to bring it into the garden.

The King was meticulous about details. He liked to write everything down in his diary or in one of his specialist day books. The weather was of absorbing interest. He had a thermometer outside his bedroom window at Royal Lodge, so that he knew the temperature the moment he got up. Little weather "stations" were dotted around the various gardens.

His wife never bothered with such

scientific data. She much preferred to stop and enquire of a trusted retainer whether he thought it would rain before she had a chance to take the cut flowers into the house. Favourites from childhood have remained lily of the valley, lemon-scented verbena, godetia, the old-fashioned single musk and damask roses. She likes to have vases of fresh flowers in her rooms, but she is not over-fond of formal arrangements. She has always found gladioli attractive—provided they are not too straight!

Like most true gardeners, Queen Elizabeth enjoys looking over other people's gardens as much as her own. In the 1950s she became Patron of the London Gardens Society and one of the least grand highlights of her year is to go visiting—to admire, to comment, and to pop inside a gardener's home for a cup of tea. Many of the people she visits are old enough to have survived one, sometimes two, world wars and there are many stories to tell of gardens destroyed and gardens restored.

Nothing will deter the Queen Mother from these annual visits. One year she arrived in appalling weather, stepped out of her car, and held out a foot to show she had come prepared—with plastic bootees over her shoes. . . .

As Patron of the London Gardens Society, the Queen Mother never misses her annual visits to some of the capital's gardens
Opposite—Top: *Every inch has been used in this South London garden*
Bottom: *Commenting on a beautiful display in a West London garden*
Top: *A delightful rockery in Greenwich*
Left: *Returning inside for a cup of tea with the owner of a garden in Camberwell*
Above: *The 'Elizabeth of Glamis' rose. This was specially developed and named after the Queen Mother by Sam McGredy, a famous rose-grower from Northern Ireland*

A daughter married

Most mothers, in matters of romance, instinctively recognise when a young daughter is in love, while many fathers fight a rear-guard action in a battle they sometimes refuse to admit is even taking place.

It seems likely that the Queen was aware long before the King, of Princess Elizabeth's feelings for the dashing naval lieutenant who came to lunch at Windsor Castle when on leave during the war. But when the King was let into the secret—or, more likely, admitted he knew what was going on—it still took some time before he was prepared to give consent to a marriage. There were good reasons for this. Practical, political reasons, and sensible hesitation by a generous and loving father. But there was also more than a hint of a last ditch defence.

Five years of war had not only deprived the Princesses of many of the joys of a more normal youth, it had also meant that the King and Queen had spent much less time with their children than they would have liked. When peace came this was one of the omissions the King intended to put right.

In September 1945 the whole family was together at Balmoral, pursuing the simple pleasures of an open-air life that all of them—Princess Margaret a shade less than the others perhaps—were so happy with. The King took particular pride in teaching

his elder daughter the skills of deerstalking. All day they would be out on the moors, pausing for a picnic lunch in the heather.

When they returned to the Castle in the evening, weary for a bath and a change of clothes, the Queen might not be there, having slipped out for an hour's fishing in the soft shade of a pool where salmon might be tempted.

But later the whole family would be gathered together round a fire, the King sipping a whisky, the Queen or Princess Margaret at the piano playing music from Bless the Bride or Annie Get Your Gun. They presented a picture, like that of so many others in Britain at the time, of a family exhausted by war but determined to catch up on lost years. The King wanted to spend as much time as possible with his daughters. He wanted to take them to the theatre, give them parties, introduce them to lots of nice young men. . . .

As most people are aware, the first proper meeting of Prince Philip and Princess Elizabeth (they had met briefly at her parents' Coronation) took place when she was only 13 and he was an 18-year-old cadet at Dartmouth Naval College. The King and Queen were having a summer holiday—the last before the war—and the King had decided it would be rather pleasant to take the royal yacht, Victoria and Albert, up the River Dart, drop anchor,

Inset left: *A somewhat demure-looking Prince Philip at the age of three*
Inset right: *Princess Elizabeth, who is five years younger than her husband, at the age of eight*
Above left: *With his parents, Prince and Princess Andrew of Greece, on an outing to the beach*
Above right: *The young Princess with her parents, the Duke and Duchess of York, at a garden party at Glamis Castle in 1931*

and go and visit his old college. The children, Elizabeth and her eight-year-old sister Margaret Rose, were to go with them.

Typically, on the actual day of the visit, it was pouring with rain. Worse, they arrived at the College to find several of the boys had gone down with mumps. This was why the two Princesses remained out of contact in the Captain's House, and how Philip came to meet Elizabeth. As a senior and uninfected cadet he was deputed to entertain the guests.

That night Philip was among the cadets entertained to dinner on the royal yacht, and the following afternoon, he was among the armada of 110 boats from the College that followed the yacht to the edge of the open sea. Indeed he clung on to the very last, and his uncle, Lord Mountbatten, at a stern rail on Victoria and Albert, watched admiringly, then turned away, muttering proudly: "Damned fool."

During the war Princess Elizabeth kept

Above: *Royal Naval College, Dartmouth*
Far right, above: *The Royal Family with Prime Minister, Field Marshal Smuts, during their South African tour in 1947*
Far right below: *Wherever the train stopped on the tour, there were always crowds waiting to see the King and Queen*
Right: *Probably the first picture of the Princess and Prince together, taken at Dartmouth Naval College in July 1939. Prince Philip, in uniform, at the back*

up a friendly correspondence with Prince Philip of Greece, as he then was, and placed a photograph of him on her mantelpiece. There is little doubt that she was in love from the start.

The Queen's attitude was to allow matters to take their natural course. All she ever wanted was her daughter's happiness, that had always had priority. But perhaps she agreed with her husband when he insisted that Elizabeth was too young and too inexperienced to think seriously of marriage to anyone at this stage.

When King George II of Greece broached the subject he received no encouragement. "We both think she is too young for that now," the British King wrote to Queen Mary in 1944, "as she has never met any young men of her own age. I like Philip. He is intelligent, has a good sense of humour and thinks about things in the right way. . . ." However, now was not ▶

Top: *The Royal Family and Prince Philip arrive at Romsey Abbey in October 1947 for the wedding of Lord Mountbatten's daughter, Patricia, to Lord Brabourne*
Above: *The engaged couple's first public appearance together at a garden party at Buckingham Palace in July 1947*
Left: *Their first official photograph after the announcement of their betrothal*

the moment. "We are going to tell George that P. had better not think any more about it for the present."

With the war's end the love between the two did not diminish—this was no wartime romance. Prince Philip was among the guests at Balmoral in 1946. Whenever he could get leave from his naval duties his sports car could be seen parked in the courtyard of Buckingham Palace. But the King still wanted Elizabeth to "meet more men", and at every opportunity eligible suitors were introduced into her company. These Guards officers, young aristocrats, and debs' delights came to be known by other members of the family as Princess Elizabeth's "bodyguard". They gave Philip no real opposition.

Gradually the round of pre-war social engagements was restored, but in nothing like its former splendour. Ascot was revived in 1946—the men in lounge suits, the ladies in day dresses with home-concocted hats. Champagne cost £3 a bottle (60/-) and strawberries and ice cream 12½p (2/6). The Times reported: "One particularly cheerless special constable, whose job was to see that people did not stand on seats, pointed out that before the war people's manners were enough to prevent them doing so."

There were garden parties once again at Buckingham Palace. Prince Philip was present at the first one, but no outsiders spotted any connection between him and the 19-year-old Princess Elizabeth.

The nation was slowly recovering from the ravages of war, but there was never to be a return to pre-war conditions. To the King's consternation the voters threw out their wartime leader Churchill, and elected Clement Attlee to be the first Labour Prime Minister since Ramsay MacDonald. "I saw Winston at 7 p.m.," wrote the King in his diary, "and it was a very sad meeting. I told him I thought the people were very ungrateful after the way they had been led in the war."

Europe had not quite settled down to peace. There was political unrest in Greece, among other places, and this complicated the question of Elizabeth possibly marrying Philip. Or rather it caused problems over the young man's desire to become a naturalised British subject.

Prince Philip was born on Corfu on June

10, 1921, the only son of Prince Andrew of Greece and Princess Alice of Battenberg. His grandfather was Prince William of Denmark, elected King of Greece. But he had lived almost entirely in England, at the home of Lord Louis Mountbatten's elder brother, the Marquess of Milford Haven, since he was eight.

The trouble was, after the civil war, the Greek people called on their King to return to Athens in 1946, and it was reckoned that it would be unhelpful if, practically at the same time, Philip renounced his Greek nationality.

The Queen felt great sympathy for her daughter. It was a shame that such political considerations should place barriers in the path of true love. But everyone would just have to continue being patient. The King was also sorry for his daughter, but perhaps he was not quite so unhappy about the delay. The Queen's close friend, Lady Airlie: "wondered sometimes whether he was secretly dreading the prospect of an early marriage." The King, in common with many other fathers, would have liked to keep both his daughters at his side for as long as possible.

As it turned out, a long-standing promise to visit South Africa provided an ideal breathing space—an opportunity for Princess Elizabeth, parted from Prince Philip for nearly four months, to be absolutely sure that she was making the right choice for her future happiness.

The Royal Family sailed from England on February 1, 1947 in HMS Vanguard, leaving behind a country shivering in near Arctic conditions. The King was so worried, especially by Press agitation for his return, that he seriously considered going home to share the ordeal with his people. But the South Africans, at that time still members of the Commonwealth, were also the Sovereign's people and to have abandoned the tour might have been a grave error.

Vanguard also had to battle with some fierce weather. Only the Queen seemed unaffected by the mountainous seas and the pitching and rolling. She continued calmly to play Chinese checkers for much of the time, gripping tightly onto the board. When the sun finally shone and the seas relented she played deck tennis energetically with her daughters—at least it took Princess Elizabeth's mind off other things. But it was noticeable that the King, always a keen sportsman and an excellent tennis player, took little part. He complained, but not often, of cramp in one leg and rested a good deal. He also had a very nasty cough, which wouldn't go away.

From February through till late April the Royal party toured 10,000 miles on the special White Train from Cape Town to Pretoria, to Johannesburg and the Rand, through the plains of the Orange Free State ▶

Above right: *Lieutenant Philip Mountbatten at the side of his future bride in a Royal Family group at Buckingham Palace*
Right: *The long-awaited wedding day— November 20, 1947*

Top: *The Royal bride and bridegroom at Buckingham Palace after the wedding*
Above: *Leaving Buckingham Palace for their honeymoon*
Right: *Enjoying a stroll in the late autumn sunshine at Broadlands*

and the sheep country of the North-East Cape. They flew to Southern Rhodesia, visited Livingstone and saw the magnificent Victoria Falls.

Some fourteen years later the South African Government was to discard its association with the Crown, and the years that followed the Royal tour have seen the African continent erupt in the cause of independence. But in the spring of 1947 there was no foreboding of these events in the warmth of the welcome given to the King and Queen by both white and black.

On April 21 Princess Elizabeth celebrated her 21st birthday, and in a radio broadcast made a solemn declaration of self-dedication to which she has remained true ever since. "It is very simple. I declare before you all that my whole life, whether it be long or short, shall be devoted to your service and the service of our great Imperial Commonwealth to which we all belong."

Along with her parents and her young sister, now a vivacious 16-year-old, Princess Elizabeth returned home delighted in the knowledge that Prince Philip's naturalisation papers had finally come through. He was now known as Lieutenant Philip Mountbatten, RN.

Both the King and Queen had become equally convinced of the young couple's deep love for one another. As Sir John Wheeler-Bennett wrote in his biography of George VI: "There could no longer be any question as to the wishes and affections of both parties, and their pertinacity and patience were rewarded."

There had been official denials of any engagement, and indeed the King kept his daughter waiting another two months before allowing the public into the secret. But when the announcement finally came it was "with the greatest pleasure that the King and Queen announce the betrothal of their dearly beloved daughter. . . ." That same evening huge crowds pressed against the railings of Buckingham Palace singing, "All the nice girls love a sailor."

The wedding, in Westminster Abbey, was to be the first in English history of an Heiress Presumptive who was later to become Queen. Characteristically, now the decision had been made, the King went about enthusiastically making the arrangements with minute attention to detail—his first remark on returning from the Abbey after the ceremony was to inquire why a certain senior admiral had turned up without his sword!

Some of the arrangements were not mere detail, however. He decided that all the expenses, with the exception of street decorations in Whitehall and the Mall, would be paid out of the Privy Purse, and he would personally foot all the housekeeping bills of the newly-weds for the first two years. He gave them a large mansion, Sunninghill Park, not far from Windsor, as a grace-and-favour home. Unfortunately, only a fortnight later it burned down, so after their honeymoon they returned to Buckingham Palace until Clarence House was made ready. He also gave his daughter diamond pendant earrings. The joint present from the King and Queen was a ruby and diamond necklace, and two pearl necklaces. Queen Mary's wedding gift was a diamond tiara, bracelets and a brooch. Princess Margaret, who as yet had few family heirlooms to pass on, gave her sister a luxuriously fitted picnic basket.

If the King was busy, so also was the Queen—as any other mother who is preparing for her first child to be married. The bridal gown, designed by Norman Hartnell, was of ivory satin, woven in Scotland, embroidered with pearls in a design of stars, roses and ears of wheat. For herself the Queen chose a magnificent dress of apricot and gold lamé, falling in cape folds at the back to a short train. Her hat was of gold lamé veiled in apricot tulle and trimmed with ostrich feathers.

The morning of the wedding dawned November cold and misty, but inside the Palace there was plenty of heat being generated. The frame of the bride's diamond tiara snapped as she was putting it on, and had to be rushed to the court jewellers for repair. Then it was discovered that her parents' present, the two pearl necklaces, had been put on display with the other wedding gifts, at St. James's Palace. A secretary was sent to recover them. Even the bride's bouquet was missing for a time—it eventually turned up in a disused cupboard.

But, thankfully, the actual service in the Abbey went without a hitch.

"Who giveth this woman?" asked the Archbishop of Canterbury, and the King, a slender figure in naval uniform, took his daughter's hand and held it forward.

"Notwithstanding the splendour and national significance of the service in this Abbey," said the Archbishop in his address, "it is in all essentials the same as it would be for any cottager who might be married this afternoon in some small country church in a remote village in the dales. The same vows are taken, the same prayers are offered. . . ."

During the honeymoon, spent at Broadlands, and Birkhall near Balmoral, Princess Elizabeth wrote a letter to her parents thanking them for all they had done. The King replied with the words of a father devoted to his daughter. "I am so glad you wrote and told Mummy that you think the long wait before your engagement . . . was for the best. I was rather afraid that you had thought I was being hard-hearted about it. . . .

"I have watched you grow up all these years with pride under the skilful direction of Mummy, who as you know, is the most marvellous person in the World in my eyes, and I can, I know, always count on you, and now Philip, to help us in our work. Your leaving us has left a great blank in our lives but do remember that your old home is still yours and do come back to it as much and as often as possible. I can see that you are sublimely happy with Philip which is right but don't forget us is the wish of

Your ever loving and devoted Papa."

Top: *Prince Philip and Princess Elizabeth spent the first part of their honeymoon at Broadlands, Hampshire, the home of Philip's uncle, Lord Mountbatten* **Inset:** *The beautifully furnished drawing room in the west wing of Broadlands* **Above and inset:** *After a weekend at Broadlands, the newly-wedded couple spent the rest of their honeymoon at Birkhall, the Queen Mother's Highland home on Deeside*

A portrait of Queen Elizabeth the Queen Mother by Sir Gerald Kelly. The painting was begun in 1939 and finally finished in 1945

Granny

The Queen's joy at learning that her daughter Princess Elizabeth was expecting her first child must have been clouded with sadness and apprehension. For the King's health was giving cause for grave concern. The tiredness which he had been unable to hide on the tour of South Africa still mysteriously plagued him.

For much of the summer of 1948 the King suffered discomfort from cramp in both legs, though exercise on the moors at Balmoral brought improvement. But by October his left foot was numb, and he was suffering a great deal of pain. Characteristically, he kept a daily record of symptoms, which he was able to hand to the doctors when they examined him.

The diagnosis was worse than anyone had anticipated. Professor James Learmouth's examination on November 12 showed the King's condition was one of early arteriosclerosis—obstruction to the circulation through hardening of the arteries. There was a danger of gangrene developing and even a strong possibility that his right leg would have to be amputated.

The examination that led to these frightening conclusions took place in the Buhl Room at Buckingham Palace, a room that had been converted to a kind of surgery. It was in this same room, only two days later, that Princess Elizabeth gave birth to her first child. On the King's strict instructions the news of his condition was kept from his daughter.

Quite naturally everyone was thrilled that Princess Elizabeth's confinement had gone so smoothly, and that she had been ▶

Above: *Queen Elizabeth proudly holds her grandson, Prince Charles, after his christening at Buckingham Palace on December 15, 1948*
Below: *The infant Prince surrounded by his godparents*
Right: *Princess Elizabeth with her first child, aged one month*

Above: *Prince Charles, aged five, plays hide-and-seek with his grandmother in the playhouse at Royal Lodge, Windsor*
Far left: *The future Queen and her husband after the christening of their son*
Left: *A somewhat haughty acknowledgement of the crowd from the balcony at Buckingham Palace brings a disapproving stare from the Princess Royal*
Below left: *Queen Mary with her first great-grandson, Prince Charles*

"delivered of a Prince at 9.14 this evening." The Queen was the first to congratulate her, after Prince Philip, and to thank her for giving her a grandchild.

At 11 p.m. on that wet November night, Queen Mary, now 81 and as erect as ever, drove to the Palace to inspect her first great-grandchild. She thought the baby looked remarkably like his great-great-great-grandfather, Prince Albert, Queen Victoria's husband. As a christening present she gave Charles a silver gilt cup and cover which George III had given to a godson in 1780: "so that I gave a present from my great-grandfather to my great-grandson 168 years later."

The christening robe of Honiton lace, worn over a satin petticoat, had been used by successive generations of the Royal Family ever since the christening of Queen Victoria's second child, Edward, in 1842.

Princess Elizabeth wrote to an old friend: "I still find it hard to believe I have a baby of my own!"

Prince Charles was one year and nine months old when his sister was born. His grandmother celebrated her 50th birthday on August 4 with her husband in London, but when the King travelled north to Balmoral a week later the Queen decided to

Left: *Prince Charles gets his share of attention after the christening of his sister, Princess Anne, on October 21, 1950*
Below: *Arriving at Ballater Station, near Balmoral, in 1951*
Inset: *The photograph of the King and his grandson that the Queen Mother still keeps near her*
Bottom: *The King, his granddaughter on his knee, with his family at Sandringham, only a few weeks before he died*

stay on for a few days to be with Princess Elizabeth. Princess Anne was born at Clarence House on August 15 at the sensible hour of 11.50 a.m.

The King's health had improved and the worry about his leg had receded. But he still had to take things carefully, and increasingly the Queen and Princess Elizabeth lifted as many of the burdens of royalty off his shoulders as he would allow.

By December 1950 Prince Philip had his own naval command—he was promoted lieutenant-commander on the same day his daughter was born—and at Christmas his wife flew out to Malta to join him, leaving their two children in the care of their grandparents at Sandringham. "Charles is too sweet, stumping around the room," the King wrote to his daughter. "We shall love having them at Sandringham. He is the fifth generation to live here and I hope he will get to like the place."

Tragically, over the next few months the King's health deteriorated once more. His wife and daughter knew, though he was never aware, that he had cancer. In October 1951, Princess Elizabeth and Prince Philip represented the King on a tour of America and Canada—the countries where he and the Queen had been so happy. Charles spent his third birthday with his grandparents. The one memory he retains of his grandfather is sitting beside him on a sofa to have a photograph taken. To this day the picture has pride of place in the Queen Mother's home.

The last farewell

King George VI waves farewell to his daughter and son-in-law as they set out from London Airport for Africa on January 31, 1952. Six nights later the King died in his sleep at Sandringham

Princess Elizabeth and Prince Philip were spending a few days at Sagana Lodge in Kenya when they received the tragic news of her father's death

He had enjoyed a perfect day's shooting on the Sandringham estate under a clear sunny sky. He had come home to a good dinner with the Queen and Princess Margaret, and had retired to his room in cheerful mood at about 10.30 after planning the next day's sport. Around midnight a security guard patrolling the grounds saw him check the latch of his bedroom window. Then the house fell silent. The following morning his valet entered the room and discovered his King had passed away peacefully during the night.

Queen Elizabeth and her daughters—even more than the King—had been aware for several months just how ill a man he was. But that did not lessen their shock at learning of his death. Members of the Household could not believe that anyone could be so brave as his widow was in the days that followed.

On the evening of his death the Queen spent several hours writing letters to friends. On the following day she came down from her room to play with her grandchildren. Her concern, as always, was for others. Her thoughts, as she knew her husband would want them to be, were for their eldest daughter, "in the great and lonely station to which she has been called."

Only seven days before, the King and Queen had taken Princess Elizabeth and Prince Philip to the theatre to see South Pacific at Drury Lane. The following morning they went to London Airport to wave the young couple off on their tour of East Africa, Australia and New Zealand—a tour which the King might have undertaken himself if he had been well enough. As it was, he had made such a good recovery from an operation on his left lung the previous year that it seemed possible he might be able to take a holiday in South Africa the following March.

However, when the public saw pictures of the King on the tarmac at Heathrow, watching the plane carrying his daughter until it was out of sight, they felt a great fear. He looked gaunt and so weary.

Princess Elizabeth and her husband were enjoying a brief respite from official receptions and staying at Sagana Lodge, a gift from the people of Kenya, when a cable brought news of her father's death. Prince Philip told his wife, and appeared if anything even more cruelly stunned than the new Queen.

Henceforth the widowed Queen would choose to be known as Queen Elizabeth the Queen Mother. Her Household were to call her Queen Elizabeth. The people were affectionately to think of her as the Queen Mother, or even the Queen Mum. Her daughter would continue to speak of her as The Queen.

The new Queen, only 25, returned to

London, a calm figure in black. And as she stepped from her plane the warrior Prime Minister, Winston Churchill, flanked by Clement Attlee and Anthony Eden, past and future Prime Ministers, bowed in homage. A little later, Queen Mary drove from Marlborough House to Clarence House. "Her old Grannie and subject," she said, "must be the first to kiss Her hand."

The courageous old lady had lived to mourn the death of three of her five sons and the abdication from the Throne of a fourth (her youngest son, John, died in 1919 and George, Duke of Kent was killed on active service in 1942). In the days to come she and the Queen Mother were to give unflinching support to the young Queen, and to reflect privately on what might have been if King Edward had not abandoned the Throne, leaving his brother to take up a task that undoubtedly drained him of strength before his time.

King George was 56 when he died, his widow 51. In other circumstances they might have looked forward to another 30 years of life together, celebrating their golden wedding anniversary as the Queen Mother's parents had done before them.

The Queen Mother was desolate with grief, but she kept her feelings under iron control as preparations were made for the funeral. At first it had been planned that the body of the King would lie in state in Westminster Hall for three days. But the period had to be extended because on the third day the queue waiting to pay homage was six abreast and stretched four miles. This was a King who in his quiet unassuming way had touched the very hearts of the ▶

Above left: *A shocked nation reads of the death of their beloved King*
Above right: *Princess Elizabeth, now Queen, arrives back in London from Kenya*
Insets: *A time of deep sorrow for the new Queen and the King's widow*
Below: *People in their thousands queued to pay their last respects at the lying-in-state of George VI*

people. The orderly grey carpet surrounding the catafalque in Westminster Hall was strewn with tiny fading bunches of spring flowers, dropped by women and children as they filed past the coffin.

Thousands slept on the pavements and sheltered in doorways on the night before the funeral. Many wept as the procession passed them the next day and the hush of silence lasted several minutes after the cortège had passed. These were men and women who had drawn strength from a King who had gone through five years of war and deprivation with them.

His widow was very aware of the love they had for him. She gave them this message: ". . . your concern for me has upheld me in my sorrow, and how proud you have made me by your wonderful tributes to my dear husband, a great and noble King. No man had a deeper sense than he of duty and of service, and no man was more full of compassion for his fellow-men. He loved you all, every one of you, most truly. That, you know, was what he always tried to tell you in his yearly message at Christmas; that was the pledge he took at the sacred moment of his Coronation 15 years ago. Now I am left alone, to do what I can to honour that pledge without him."

In 1955, when King George VI's daughter unveiled his memorial statue in London's Mall, she used these words.

"Much was asked of my father in personal sacrifice and endeavour, often in the face of illness; his courage . . . endeared him to everyone. He shirked no task, however difficult, and to the end he never faltered in his duty. . . . Throughout all the strains of his public life he remained a man of warm and friendly sympathies—a man who by simple qualities of loyalty, resolution and service won for himself such a place in the affection of all of us that when he died millions mourned for him as a true and trusted friend. . . ."

Opposite—**Top:** *Mourners pay silent tribute at the lying-in-state of George VI in Westminster Hall*
Centre: *The Duke of Edinburgh, Duke of Windsor, Duke of Gloucester and Duke of Kent at the start of the sad journey to Windsor Castle*
Bottom: *Three Queens—Queen Elizabeth II, Queen Mary and Queen Elizabeth the Queen Mother—in mourning for George VI*
Below: *The funeral procession moves solemnly through Windsor Castle to St. George's Chapel*

The Queen's Coronation

Following the precedent set by Queen Mary, it was decided that the Queen Mother should attend the Coronation of her daughter. And as the preparations went ahead she was able, from her own experience, to give advice about important details that might otherwise have given additional worry to the young Queen.

Sadly, Queen Mary was not to live to see the great day. This magnificent, formidable lady—"talking to her was like talking to St. Paul's Cathedral"—had been too weak to attend the funeral of George VI, and she let it be known that her own death should not be allowed to affect the celebration of the Coronation in any way. Her last days passed sedately at Marlborough House, her friend of so many years, Lady Airlie, beside her always.

Queen Mary died on March 24, 1953, just a little over a year after the death of her son, and a little less than three months before the Coronation of her devoted granddaughter.

Winston Churchill, that other great battler, was still alive. And as he promised the country, Coronation Day was going to be: "A day the oldest are proud to have lived to see, and the youngest will remember all their lives."

The procession was going to be so long it would take 45 minutes to pass. Two thousand bandsmen, in 46 bands, would either be in the procession or stationed along the route. The Ministry of Works was issuing 110,000 Coronation cushions—"the property of the Ministry for the use of spectators"—but wasn't at all sure what would happen to them afterwards.

The newspapers ran stories about the Sheffield man who had portraits of the Queen and Prince Philip in full regalia tattooed on each shoulder; about the 15 women in Glasgow who were scrubbing down the walls and pavements in their street to make it the cleanest in the city; about the pub that was selling beer at the pre-war price of 2½p a pint. A noted MP was widely quoted as saying she did not know what all the fuss was about—"I hope it's the last Coronation this country will ever see"—and Sir Harold Scott, Metropolitan Police Commissioner warned: "When you are glued to the TV screen watch out there is no-one upstairs robbing the house."

This was to be the first post-war spectacle—after the Queen's wedding—and in addition to the 100,000 who lined the procession route there were to be millions watching the ceremony on nine-inch television screens—either their own, or more likely, neighbours' sets, because television was still an expensive luxury.

June 2, 1953 was a day of magnificent pageantry and rejoicing. A day that rightly belonged to the Queen. But while the television cameras concentrated on the moving ceremony at the altar steps, now and again there would be a shot of the Queen Mother and Princess Margaret, seated in their place of honour in the front row of the Royal Gallery.

Wearing a robe of purple velvet, with a stiff white satin dress, and jewels that ▶

Above: *The newly-crowned Queen sits on King Edward's Chair before returning to her Throne to receive homage from her peers*
Inset: *Even the rehearsal of the Coronation procession attracted enthusiastic crowds*

included a triple diamond necklace, the Queen Mother looked composed, reflective, and much younger than 52. For the first time in many years she was the spectator rather than the centre of attention. For once the limelight was diverted elsewhere. But not entirely so. . . .

About 45 minutes after the service had begun there was a tiny commotion in the Royal Gallery as Mrs. Helen Lightbody, nannie to the Queen, guided Prince Charles into the pew to a place between his grandmother and his aunt.

Early on in the preparations it had been decided that the heir to the Throne would not attend the Coronation, even though, as Duke of Cornwall, he was a senior royal duke. At four-and-a-half years of age he was not usually very good in church, developing the fidgets after approximately 10 to 15 minutes.

But he and Princess Anne had caught something of the pre-Coronation excitement. They had seen their parents trying on their robes and had watched and heard all the marching and shouting of soldiers and their commanding officers. Charles begged to be allowed to go to the Abbey. Eventually

Above left: *Prince Charles keeps asking questions, eager to learn from his granny about all that's happening. Aunt Margaret is on his left*
Above right: *The Coronation ceremony is over and Queen Elizabeth the Queen Mother walks in procession through the Abbey*
Left: *To the deafening cheers of thousands, the Queen and her Consort return home*

Left: *Towns and villages all over the country held street parties to celebrate*
Above: *Commemorative souvenirs of Coronation Day*
Below: *The Queen poses with her maids of honour after returning from the Abbey*

the Queen relented, and so, as soon as he had seen his mother and father drive out of the Palace gates in the State Coach of George III, Prince Charles—but not his sister—was spruced up in a white satin suit, his hair was slicked down, and he and Nanny Lightbody were driven by a circuitous route to a side door of the great church.

It must have been the cause of some puzzlement to him, once he was inside and peeping over the ledge of the Gallery, to see that while everyone else was dressed in crimson and purple and looking very regal, his mother was wearing the plainest white robe. By chance he had arrived at about that moment in the service when the Sovereign is anointed with consecrated oil.

He may have been puzzled, but he was not bored. He kept up a barrage of whispered questions, to which the Queen Mother bent down to give whispered answers and general commentary. She was very keen that her grandson should remember this day all his life.

Charles expressed particular interest in the size of a piece of gold plate on the altar, and also the smell of the hair oil Nanny Lightbody had used. He kept smoothing his head, then offering his palm to Granny to smell. Despite this, he lasted out well, and was allowed to stay for longer than had been planned.

When the Queen returned to Buckingham Palace after the long and tiring ceremony, she and Prince Philip stepped out onto the balcony in response to the wild cheering of the thousands of well-wishers gathered below. Then Prince Philip led out their two children, and the cheering grew even louder. But perhaps the greatest cheer of all was reserved for the moment when he brought forward Queen Elizabeth the Queen Mother, a small gracious figure who stood surrounded by her family, the centre and the core.

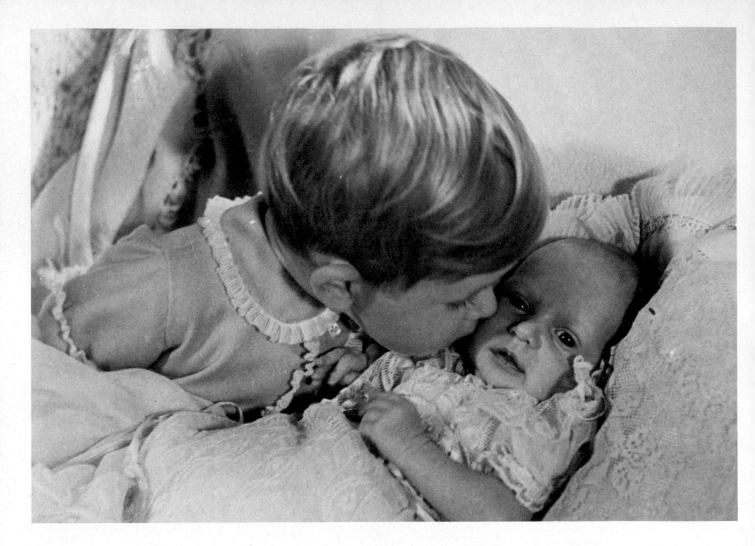

My first grandchildren

When Prince Charles was a child of three his grandmother impressed on him that he must always bow when he entered a room where his grandparents, the King and Queen, were sitting—something of which Queen Mary certainly approved. She herself liked her great-grandchildren, after she had offered a cheek to be pecked, to remain standing while they were in her presence. At least the Queen Mother never went as far as that! But she did believe in children being brought up not only to respect their elders, but even within the Royal Family, to show proper courtesy to the Sovereign.

The King should also act as King, even when his inclination was to catch hold of his grandson when he came flying into the room and swing him round in his arms.

Perhaps it was a slightly old-fashioned notion (from the first the Queen and Prince Philip gave instructions that Charles and Anne were not to bow and curtsy to them), but if any barrier was formed between the Prince and his grandparents as a result, it has never been apparent.

Ever since he can remember, Prince Charles has thought of his grandmother as just about the most wonderful person in the world. And she, it is probably true to say, regards him as her favourite grandchild. She sees in Charles the same qualities of gentleness and concern for others that she so admired in King George VI. Also, in a sense, he is the son she never had.

Prince Charles grew up especially close to the Queen Mother and the feelings of mutual affection were there from the start. His maternal grandfather had died before he was four and his paternal grandfather had died in Monte Carlo before Charles was born. His paternal grandmother, Princess Alice, founded a religious order and only came to Buckingham Palace towards the end of her life, where she died in 1969.

One of Charles' first public engagements took place just after his fourth birthday. He accompanied his grandmother to one of Sir Robert Mayer's concerts for children at the Royal Festival Hall.

Eighteen months later the Queen Mother took both Charles and Anne down to Portsmouth and saw them off on the royal yacht Britannia. They were going to meet their parents in the Mediterranean at the end of the great six-month Commonwealth tour that the Queen made following her Coronation.

Remembering how she, when Duchess of York, had missed the early months of her daughter's development through being abroad, the Queen Mother spent every spare minute with her two grandchildren while the Queen was away. Among the presents she bought Charles was a miniature set of gardening tools, but if they were meant to fire a lasting interest in horticulture they must be deemed a failure. Pointing the way to much greater success was the purchase of Princess Anne's first saddle—a fourth birthday present.

Even when both were small children, the Queen Mother perceived with a granny's eye just how different in temperament were Charles and Anne. Today brother and sister understand and appreciate one another much more than they used to—right up ▶

Above: *One of the pictures from Princess Anne's first official "sitting" in .*
September 1950
Right: *Spending the day with their grandmother at Royal Lodge, Windsor*

Watching the Highland Games at Braemar with other members of the Royal Family

A rather disgruntled Charles leads the way to a ringside seat at Windsor

The Queen Mother takes Charles and Anne to see their father play polo

Deep in conversation with his grandmother at the start of another polo match

until shortly before Anne was married they did not have a great deal in common.

As a small boy the Queen Mother saw how nervous and shy Charles was, how worried he could be about doing the wrong thing—just like his grandfather used to be. Anne, on the other hand, was always much more self-assured, much more outgoing—just like her father.

It is perhaps misleading to say that Charles was the more sensitive of the two, when really it might have been simply that Anne, like most girls, matured more quickly. But she was always much less likely than her brother to run to granny when she fell over and grazed a knee, or ask for her support when she and Charles quarrelled. Princess Anne was the bossy one, the Queen Mother could see, and although she never showed favouritism it was clear to her, as it was to others, that Charles would need very careful handling if he was to grow out of his shyness and gain self-confidence.

Both the Queen Mother and her daughters had been educated at home by governesses. But when it came to deciding about the education of their son, the Queen and Prince Philip came to the conclusion it would be best if the heir to the Throne was given the opportunity of mixing with other children as early as possible.

At the age of eight he was sent to a private school in Knightsbridge, and on his first day had to run the gauntlet of photographers and reporters. From there he went on as a boarder to Cheam, his father's old preparatory school, and was fairly miserable for much of the time, missing home dreadfully.

The question of where he should go from there was frequently discussed within the Royal Family. The Queen Mother sided with the Queen in believing Eton was the natural choice. But Prince Philip strongly favoured Gordonstoun. Charles, who was consulted on the matter, thought the idea of a spartan life in the north of Scotland sounded "fairly gruesome". But as his father pointed out: "It's near Balmoral. There's always the Factor there; you can go and stay with him. And your grandmother goes up there to fish. You can go and see her."

The final outcome was fairly predictable, as in family matters Prince Philip was very much the head. And, in any case, the Queen confessed to being somewhat mystified by all the pros and cons of various public schools.

Prince Charles looks back on his early days at Gordonstoun with a profound sense of gratitude to the Queen Mother. She very soon realised how lonely and homesick he was, how difficult he found it to emulate the sporting prowess his father had shown as a pupil at Gordonstoun.

When he visited her at Birkhall, her home on the Balmoral estate, the Queen Mother offered sympathy, gave her grandson the sort of food he liked and cheered him up no end. But when he hesitantly asked her to intercede with his parents to be moved to another school, she firmly declined. She would give him all the support she could, ▶

Princess Anne accompanies her grandmother to the Trooping the Colour ceremony in 1966

At the Badminton Horse Trials—an event Anne would later excel in

MY FIRST GRANDCHILDREN *continued*

but he must stick to the task. Things would get better—and they did.

"He is a very gentle boy, with a very kind heart," she said at about this time, "which I think is the essence of everything."

When she saw her grandson during his first term at his next school—Timbertop, in Australia, 200 miles north of Melbourne—the change in him was marvellous. The 17-year-old Prince Charles was given leave to meet the Queen Mother in Canberra, during her Australian visit, and together they spent two wonderfully carefree days driving through the Snowy Mountains, sharing a cabin at River Bend, and exchanging news of school and home. The Queen Mother was so delighted to see how happy Charles was that she had no hesitation in recommending to his parents that he should stay on at Timbertop for a second term.

Princess Anne was very jealous of her brother when he went away to his first boarding school. The thought of leaving home held no terrors for her apparently. And, once he'd gone, she found she missed his company.

She had to battle on from the age of five until 12 with lessons from tutors at Buckingham Palace. But at last, in the autumn of 1963, she became a boarder herself, at Benenden. The Queen arrived with her daughter from Scotland, and 320 girls were gathered outside to greet the new pupil. By all accounts, Princess Anne settled in very quickly and easily. She was popular with staff and fellow pupils, showing little of the strong will that was to annoy some in later years.

Three generations at the Braemar Highland Games in 1964

The Queen Mother on her 60th birthday, with her third grandchild, Prince Andrew, and Princess Anne

A painful decision

In the light of subsequent events, it would be particularly interesting to discover whether the Queen Mother now thinks Princess Margaret should have married Group Captain Peter Townsend in 1955. The last 25 years have seen a radical change in attitudes and perhaps there are many more people today who believe it is really no business of anyone outside the Royal Family what an individual member thinks or does—especially in matters of love.

In 1944 Peter Townsend, at the age of 30, was a handsome RAF fighter pilot whom King George VI had chosen to be one of his equerries. The King was anxious to have about him men who had distinguished themselves in battle.

And from the very beginning Peter Townsend was popular with the whole of the Royal Family. He was charming, efficient at his job, and able to fit into the private life of the King and Queen without awkwardness or hint of sycophancy. The King enjoyed his company, and saw

nothing untoward in his respectful friendship with his daughters. For one thing he was twice the age of his youngest daughter. And for another, he was married, with children of his own.

The Queen, too, liked the Group Captain. His sympathetic manner, his almost poetic turn of phrase appealed to her romantic nature. When she worried so much about her husband's illness she was able to turn to him for comfort and support.

Indeed, she thought so highly of the royal equerry that after the King's death, the Queen Mother appointed him her Comptroller when she moved to Clarence House with Princess Margaret. Her feelings were reciprocated. "My admiration and affection for Queen Elizabeth," wrote the Group Captain in his recent autobiography, "was, like everybody's, boundless—all the more so because beneath her graciousness, her gaiety and her unfailing thoughtfulness for others she possessed a steely will."

Whether it was a steely will, or whether—more likely—it was because of the strict

moral·standards to which she has adhered all her life, the Queen Mother must have been painfully troubled by the discovery, shortly before the Coronation, that her youngest daughter and the Group Captain were very much in love and wished to marry.

By now, Peter Townsend had been granted a divorce from his wife on the grounds of her adultery. But however much the Queen Mother, and the Queen, wished to please Princess Margaret—and both have always loved her very dearly and desired the greatest happiness for her—there were tremendous obstacles to granting her permission to marry the man she loved.

When consulted, the Prime Minister, Winston Churchill, advised the Queen that a marriage between her only sister and a divorced servant of the Royal Family was ▶

Above: *Peter Townsend walks before the King and Queen outside Parliament House in Cape Town during the Royal tour of 1947*

Above: *By now a constant companion, Peter Townsend stands behind Princess Margaret and other members of the Royal Family during Ascot Week, 1952*
Left: *With the 19-year-old Princess*

out of the question, especially at the start of a new reign. He insisted, with Press reports of the tiniest details building the situation into a major scandal, that Peter Townsend must be sent abroad. The Queen and the Queen Mother reluctantly agreed. Townsend himself had already volunteered to go away. He was given an appointment as air attaché at the British Embassy in Brussels. From there Princess Margaret and he could still write and telephone one another, but they were not to meet.

The Queen Mother has never been one to hurry over important decisions. She is a strong believer in the steadying influence of time. But if in fact her private wish was that her daughter should eventually marry the man she loved, then she had an ally in the Royal Marriages Act of 1772, under which those in line of succession to the Throne have to secure the Sovereign's consent if they wish to marry before the age of 25. After that age they still have to seek permission, but only for an additional period of 12 months.

Princess Margaret was 23 in 1953. She had two years, three years at the most, to wait before she would be allowed to marry Peter.

Of course it was not the Queen Mother's permission that Princess Margaret had to seek, but in a family matter such as this mother and daughter would have sought one another's advice. And all three women would have asked themselves: what would King George have wished?

The problem was that the Margaret-Townsend affair, as it came to be known, had not remained a family matter. To the world's Press, and its readers, it had become a love story that few could resist. Older people feared a repetition of the Edward VIII and Mrs. Simpson crisis, though there was very little comparison—for one thing Princess Margaret was not the heir to the Throne. The young and the romantic tended to hope the couple would marry, with or without permission, and thereby cock a snook at the over-stuffy Establishment.

For a time, unaware of the letter writing and phone calls that were passing between the Group Captain and the Princess, the public believed the love affair might indeed have quietly ended.

But when Peter Townsend arrived back in England in October 1955, some seven

Above: *With his eldest son, Giles, at a Windsor gymkhana*
Right: *Accompanying the King and Queen at the International Horse Show, 1947*

Top: *After a two-year separation, Peter Townsend sees Princess Margaret again at Clarence House in October 1955*
Above: *With his second wife, the Belgian tobacco heiress Marie-Luce, whom he married in 1959, and their three children*
Right: *At the Badminton Horse Trials*

weeks after Princess Margaret's 25th birthday, and they met the next evening at Clarence House, Press interest soared once more. An American newspaper discovered that the Queen Mother had joined them for tea at one of their many subsequent meetings, and ran the uproarious headline: "Meg sips tea with Peter. Mom makes it a crowd."

The Queen Mother, like her own mother, is not a person to be harsh on her children. And she doesn't lose her temper. She listens to all arguments, takes time to make up her mind, then rarely changes it. It seems very likely that in the end the Queen Mother could not approve of a marriage between her youngest daughter and Group Captain Peter Townsend. There were too many arguments against it. But she relied on

Princess Margaret coming to the same conclusion on her own, in her own time.

The Queen desperately wanted her sister to have a free choice, but there was so much opposition from within the Cabinet, and seemingly from a large section of the public, that it appeared less and less likely that she would receive general approval to marry.

And if Margaret did decide to go ahead and marry Townsend, she and the Queen learned late in October from the Prime Minister, then she would have to renounce her rights to the succession, retire from royal life, and surrender the £15,000 a year she was entitled to on marriage.

"There would be nothing left—except me," wrote Peter Townsend in his autobiography, "and I hardly possessed the

weight to compensate for the loss of her privy purse and prestige. It was too much to ask of her, too much for her to give. We should be left with nothing but our devotion to face the world."

On October 31, 25 years ago, Princess Margaret issued a statement from Clarence House an hour after she had said a last farewell to the man she loved. It contained high-minded phrases like "conscious of my duty to the Commonwealth" and "mindful of the Church's teaching that Christian marriage is indissoluble". It was stiff and it was proper, but everything that really mattered to the Princess personally, the irrevocable decision, was in the first words: "I would like it to be known that I have decided not to marry Group Captain Townsend."

Castle of Mey

*The Queen Mother enjoys the evening sunshine
with her corgis outside her Highland home*

The Castle of Mey, standing resolute on a wind-scourged corner of Caithness, in the far north of Scotland, is the Queen Mother's prized possession, the one house she bought and paid for out of her own money. She loves every nook and cranny of it.

She came upon the castle almost by accident, and when she acquired her new home many thought it signalled the end of her public life. It was geographically so far removed from any of the other royal residences, and the purchase was made at a particularly sad time.

In the weeks following her husband's death, when reaction had set in and she was feeling desperately lonely and uncertain, the Queen Mother went to stay with old friends at their home on the Caithness coast. One afternoon, while they were out

for a drive, they paid a visit to the ancient and tumbled-down Barrogill Castle, which had been up for sale for some time without attracting a buyer. Her hosts told the Queen Mother it was likely that the castle would be demolished. "Never!" she protested. "I'll buy it."

And so she did, and changed the name back to what it had been when an Earl of Caithness rebuilt it 400 years ago. "I felt a great wish to preserve, if I could, this ancient dwelling."

Perhaps the original reason behind buying the Castle was, subconsciously, to have somewhere to hide away in her utter desolation. But very soon the old building, with its neglected garden and surrounding acres of austere landscape stretching to a rugged coastline, revitalised her.

"It is a delight to me now that I have a

home in Caithness," she told the citizens of Wick on receiving the freedom of their town. "A county of such great beauty, combining as it does, the peace and tranquillity of an open and uncrowded countryside with the rugged glory of a magnificent coastline—the remote detachment of country villages with the busy and independent life of your market towns."

Making the Castle of Mey habitable took a good deal of time, and cost a considerable amount of money. But no-one could say, seeing it fully restored, that the effort was in any way an extravagance. The Queen Mother took such loving care over every detail of its restoration. Because several of the rooms are small, much of her own furniture would not fit in. So over a period she has acquired some fine pieces at auctions. The whole place needed rewiring

The ancient Castle of Mey, proud on the northern shore of the Scottish mainland, its tranquil air in sharp contrast to the surrounding harsh landscape of Caithness. Beyond the castle turrets lie the wild and stormy seas of the Pentland Firth—on a clear day the views are magnificent

and central heating had to be installed.

When it came to decoration the Queen Mother favoured a combination of warm-coloured furnishings and white walls, and left the stone-flagged floors of the hall and staircase partly covered with coconut matting. Her own sitting room is in one of the towers. With barrel-vaulted ceiling and thick walls, it is made cosy by chintz-covered easy chairs and a Stuart tartan fireside rug.

The Castle has been in the Queen Mother's care now for over a quarter of a century, and eventually it may well pass on to Prince Charles who shares with his grandmother a love for open Scottish countryside and views of wide expanse of sea. There is good salmon fishing to be had on the Thurso River, and fine walks along the wide sweep of deserted sandy beach.

Perhaps the Queen Mother has not managed to escape to her beloved Mey as often as she would have liked, but life in that part of the world is so totally different from life in the south that within a few minutes of arriving cares slip away as lightly as a silk shawl. Though the wind blows almost incessantly, the warm Gulf Stream flowing along the coast allows flowers and fruit to flourish inside the high-walled garden, which has been cultivated to perfection. And on a long summer's evening, when it stays light till almost midnight, to sit on a bench against the stout walls of the castle and watch the blaze of sunset is wondrously peaceful.

The people of Caithness—the Castle lies a few miles to the west of John o' Groat's—love having the Queen Mother among them; hearing her talk about The Swirlies and The Twirlies—the names the locals ▶

Top left and above: *A richly-embroidered tapestry of the Queen Mother's coat of arms contrasts well with the simplicity of the decoration in the dining room*
Top right: *The blackamoor statue stands in a niche at the top of the stairs beside one of the many antique clocks*
Right: *The hallway opens straight on to a majestic divided staircase*
Opposite: *The welcoming entrance to the Castle. The tree on the left is one of two planted by George VI's grandparents while on a visit to Thurso in the 1870s*

*Opposite–***Above:** *Looking down from the top of the divided staircase to the hall*
Below: *The drawing room reflects the Queen Mother's love of pastel colours*

Above: *The Royal Family arrive for tea with "Granny" at Castle of Mey*
Right: *Chatting with the Minister of Canisbay after the Sunday morning service*

give to the two famous whirlpools on the Pentland Firth; seeing her pop in and out of Thurso shops. They would never dream of intruding on her privacy, any more than she would on theirs, but they are pleased that she takes such an interest in all their goings-on, glad that she feels so "at home" with them.

On Sundays she worships in the tiny whitewashed church of Canisbay, sitting in the pew of the Earls of Caithness, and lingering at the door afterwards to chat with the minister and hear the latest news from neighbours.

The rest of the Royal Family regard the Castle of Mey very much as the Queen Mother's private retreat, where she can get away from them all for a while. But it has become a tradition that in August, when the Queen and her family sail in Britannia up through the Western Isles and round the tip of Scotland, weather permitting, they always drop anchor in Thurso Bay, come ashore and drive over to see "Granny". Princess Margaret, Princess Anne and the Queen Mother all have birthdays in August and they like to celebrate in Scotland, often at Mey.

There is always a splendid lunch and a sumptuous tea and, best of all, no sightseers or marauding photographers. It is an ideal family day, in a perfect family setting.

Jewellery

Few women can wear jewellery to such good effect as Queen Elizabeth the Queen Mother. When she appears in the Royal Box at the Royal Opera House or attends a state banquet she manages to combine and convey to all present a sense of grace and stupendous regal splendour. From long experience she knows precisely what to wear on each occasion, and she never disappoints—though she may make envious—those she wishes to please.

Her favourite pieces of jewellery, not surprisingly, are those given to her by her family, particularly the magnificent gems presented to her by her husband over the years. There is a naval cap badge, depicted in diamonds, which he gave to her at the time of their engagement; and the necklace of diamonds and pearls, with a pendant to match, which was his wedding present to her. Just after his Coronation he produced a jewelled Thistle Badge and Star, which he had secretly prepared because there was only one in the Crown Jewels collection. "I wear it one night, the Queen the next," he joked.

The crown that she wore at King George VI's Coronation was specially made, and displayed the Koh-i-Noor diamond which had been removed from Queen Mary's crown. The four diamond-studded arches can be detached, leaving a circlet which the Queen Mother has worn on several occasions, including the ceremony of her daughter's Coronation.

The Queen Mother has access at times to certain of the Crown Jewels, but she also has a large collection of personal jewellery. One item which she wears frequently is a honeycomb tiara, with star tips standing above the main design. Originally given to Queen Mary it is set with magnificent South African diamonds.

The total value of the Queen Mother's jewellery would be impossible to calculate because no part of it is ever likely to come on the open market. Most pieces have been passed down from one generation to the next, and the practice is likely to continue.

Jewellery is important to the Queen Mother as a woman. She enjoys setting it off against the colours of the dress she is wearing, whether it be a ball gown or a short dress. She has some beautiful and priceless pearl necklaces, but also a large collection of lapel brooches, which she wears just because she likes them, or, quite often, because they have a special connection with the people or place she is going to visit. The Queen Mother is not a vain woman, but she cares about the way she looks—if people are going to be looking at her, as they always are—and she wants to look *right*.

Jewellery suits the Queen Mother, whether she wears a simple, but delicate lapel brooch, one of her favourite three-stranded pearl necklaces, or a complete set of diamonds and rubies, as she did for the Cecil Beaton portrait, top right. An exquisite diamond and pearl brooch, above right, was originally given to Queen Victoria on her Diamond Jubilee by the members of her Household. The magnificent Star, below right, is part of the insignia of the Most Noble Order of the Garter, which King George VI conferred on his wife in 1936

A portrait by Stanley Cursiter, at 60, for the Royal College of Physicians of Edinburgh, of which the Queen Mother is an Honorary Fellow

Princess Margaret

Along with the great majority of people in Britain, everyone in the Royal Family has always wished that Princess Margaret should find lasting happiness, though, it has to be said, one or two may have found their patience sorely tried from time to time.

The Queen Mother has never been anything but patient and compassionate, doing her best to consider everyone's point of view. She has strong views on moral standards, but realises that times have changed. She doesn't try to mould people, she looks for the good in them—which means she doesn't always see the bad until it is too late. Then she feels let down.

She knows her own younger daughter possibly better than anyone, and is aware that she would never deliberately do anything to hurt the feelings of her mother.

Even as children Princess Margaret and her sister were different in character. The one mischievous, witty, romantically inclined; the other, though not at all lacking in

Top: *The Queen Mother joins her daughter and future son-in-law for an informal engagement photograph in the grounds of Royal Lodge, Windsor*

After signing the register, the newly-married couple begin the procession towards the west door of the Abbey

a sense of humour, more serious in every way. When their father unexpectedly came to the Throne, Elizabeth seemed better able to cope with being "the King's daughter". She was heir to the Throne, she knew where her future lay.

Margaret, one suspects, has often had periods of doubt about her own role—"younger daughter of the King", "the Queen's sister". She has none of the defined responsibilities of the monarch, but few freedoms either. Hers is an unenviable position in many ways, and the Queen Mother must be grateful that the Queen has been such a staunch and loving friend to her sister in the emotional crises she has had to contend with.

When, nearly five years after her break with Peter Townsend, (who married a 20-year-old Belgian heiress in 1959), Princess Margaret announced her engagement to Antony Armstrong-Jones, the public was taken by surprise, but delighted for them both. The news, coming as it did just a week after the birth of Prince Andrew—the first child of what was to be called the Queen's "second family"—seemed a good omen at the start of a new decade.

Tony Armstrong-Jones, with his photographer's studio in Pimlico, his informal dress—though never on formal occasions—and his generally artistic outlook was welcomed. The next 10 years, after all, were going to become known as the Swinging Sixties. Above all, the fact that he was a commoner who earned his own living was in keeping with the times. He was well out of the usual run of bridegrooms for royal brides. The Queen Mother was greatly taken with him from the start.

The wedding, at Westminster Abbey on May 6, 1960, was a particularly joyous event because everyone felt Princess Margaret deserved the best after all the unhappiness she had suffered. She was 29 years old, but looked even younger—a tiny figure in a dress of silk organza with a tight bodice and long, close-fitting sleeves. She had eight bridesmaids, chief among them being a slightly nervous-looking Princess Anne, aged nine. Some 2,000 guests attended the wedding, and millions more joined in by watching the first live television coverage of a royal wedding.

As the married couple progressed down the aisle, there was an especially touching moment as they paused, he to bow, she to curtsy to the Queen and the Queen Mother, surely two of the happiest women in the huge congregation.

During the wedding breakfast at Buckingham Palace, a mass of well-wishers pressed towards the Palace railings, breaking the police cordon, and chanting: "We want Margaret . . . We want Tony." When the bride and bridegroom set off for their honeymoon in an open Rolls Royce, several of the guests, led by Princess Anne and followed closely by the Queen Mother, ran after the car through the courtyard, showering rose petals.

The royal yacht Britannia took Princess Margaret and her husband on a cruise ▶

The marriage took place on a perfect spring morning. The simplicity of the bride's gown contrasted with the frilled and tucked bridesmaids' dresses. At Princess Margaret's request these were based on an evening dress much liked by her father and the first one that Norman Hartnell designed for her as a young girl of 17

A family send-off for the honeymoon couple

to the Caribbean for their honeymoon. On one of the islands they visited they were shown a plot of land given as a wedding present by an old friend of the Princess, Colin Tennant. This island, which was to figure so large in the gossip columns in the following years, was Mustique.

Tony Armstrong-Jones was given the title of Lord Snowdon in 1961, and in the same year, on November 3, Princess Margaret presented him with a son, David Albert Charles, Viscount Linley of Nymans. He was the Queen Mother's third grandson and fourth grandchild, and he was born under her own roof at Clarence House.

Four years after her wedding, almost to the day, Princess Margaret and Lord Snowdon's second child, Lady Sarah Frances Elizabeth was born.

But the marriage that was welcomed as being out of the usual mould for royal marriages was mysteriously criticised after a while, notably in sections of the Press, for the very same reason. An excellent photographer and documentary film maker in his own right, Lord Snowdon was none the less accused of taking advantage of his special position—something which he took pains not to do. "I am not a member of the Royal Family," he often said. "I married a member of the Royal Family, which is quite different."

Princess Margaret enjoyed the company of her husband's friends, the artists, designers, and the high-tension life they led. But she also liked it to be understood, sometimes on the most relaxed and informal occasions, that she was a royal Princess, the sister of the Queen. She adored her husband, but the fact that he was determined to have a life and a career outside the round of royal duties irked her. Both of them were volatile, prone to rages, and increasingly they found they were happier when they were apart, pursuing their own interests. Even their children, whom they both loved deeply, could not in the end keep them together.

The separation in March 1976—the same week that Harold Wilson announced his

Happy times at Ascot 1963

Setting out for an evening engagement

Above: *After morning service with their two children, David and Sarah*
Right: *Princess Margaret accompanying her mother to Trooping the Colour, 1979*
Below left: *Flowers for Granny from her youngest grandchildren on her 70th birthday*
Below right: *Signs of strain at the Badminton Horse Trials, 1972*

intention to retire from his premiership— did not create a furore. It was something, sadly, which was happening in so many marriages. Both the Queen and the Queen Mother accepted the situation and went out of their way to help Princess Margaret and Lord Snowdon through the crisis.

Lord Snowdon remains a good friend of the Queen Mother—he is welcome at all family gatherings—and Princess Margaret and her children, (she has custody), spend a great deal of time at Clarence House. Indeed, the children look on the Queen Mother's London residence practically as their second home.

The Queen Mother is the kind of person who will do almost anything, forgive almost anything, to prevent a family unit disintegrating altogether. And she is not just thinking of protecting the image of royalty. Family life and family love have always meant everything to her.

Royal Lodge

The pink-washed elegance of Royal Lodge, Windsor Great Park

Left: *Family tea at Royal Lodge in 1950, a painting by James Gunn.*
Top: *Royal Chapel, Windsor.* **Above:** *The miniature Welsh cottage*

Queen Elizabeth the Queen Mother has four homes: Clarence House in London, overlooking the Mall and only a three-minute drive from Buckingham Palace; Birkhall, a dower house on the Balmoral estate where the Queen Mother has made it a tradition to give summer parties to her grandchildren and their friends each year; the Castle of Mey, the home in Caithness which she saved from destruction; and Royal Lodge, in Windsor Great Park. Of all, the last is no doubt her favourite home. She has spent so much time there, over a period of nearly 50 years, that the house is crammed with memories, most of them happy ones.

It was King George V who introduced her to the house, in 1931, when she was Duchess of York. He took his daughter-in-law and the Duke of York over to see it one afternoon when they were staying at Windsor Castle. They had been mildly complaining about the lack of privacy at their London house, 145 Piccadilly, and wishing they had somewhere to escape to at weekends. Well, thought the King, the Royal Lodge might be just the ticket. And so it turned out to be.

The Duchess was enraptured by the possibilities presented at her first sight of the dilapidated house and wilderness of a garden. The Duke was slightly less enthusiastic—an awful lot of work needed to be done—but he was none the less grateful to his father, and pleased for his wife. He knew that the children, Elizabeth and Margaret Rose, would be excited at the prospect of a house with such a big garden to play in.

"It is too kind of you to have offered us Royal Lodge," the Duke wrote to his father, who replied that he was pleased they liked it, but he hoped they would call it "*The* Royal Lodge, by which name it has been known ever since George IV built it. There can be any number of Royal Lodges, but only one known as The Royal Lodge." (The Duke of York stuck to his father's wishes, but over the years the prefix has been dropped and plain Royal Lodge is today more commonly used.)

Although George IV did build the basis of the present Royal Lodge, there had been a house on the site some 100 years before that, the first recorded being a large pink-walled cottage with a white porch and green shutters. This house was known as Lower Lodge to distinguish it from the Great Lodge, where the Duke of Cumberland, son of George II lived for a time. Lower Lodge was the home for many years of one Thomas Sandby, Deputy Ranger of Windsor Great Park in the early 18th century, and brother of Paul Sandby, the artist.

(In 1959 one of Paul Sandby's water-colours of the house came up for auction in London. The Queen Mother wanted to bid, but when she learned that her daughter had already instructed an agent to do so, she regretfully withdrew. The following Christmas the painting was a surprise present from the Queen to her mother. It now has pride of place in the Queen Mother's drawing room.)

The Prince Regent, who became George IV, used Lower Lodge while the Great Lodge was being prepared for him. He felt he just had to get away from his father, George III, who was quietly going mad in Windsor Castle. But when the poor old King eventually died George IV decided to start all over again by pulling down Lower Lodge and erecting an imposing edifice with no fewer than three libraries and a wide verandah running almost all the way round the house.

George IV had a positive mania for building, but Royal Lodge, like so many of his grandiose plans, was never fully completed. This was the king, it should be remembered, who rarely got up till six in the evening, went to bed again at 10, and called for a valet in the middle of the night to read the time on his bedside watch.

His brother, William IV, would never have been the cause of any such extravagant nonsense. For economy's sake he pulled down part of George's Royal Lodge—times were so hard he tried to get rid of the new, unfinished Buckingham Palace. After Queen Victoria had used it as a place to take tea on drives round Windsor Great Park, ▶

Top: *When at Windsor, the Queen Mother works at her desk in the Octagon Room*
Above: *In the grounds of Royal Lodge on her 70th birthday*

the Lodge eventually became the grace-and-favour residence of first a Comptroller to the Lord Chamberlain, and secondly Edward VII's racing manager.

The outstanding feature of Royal Lodge remains the Saloon, which measures a gigantic 48 feet long, 29 feet wide, and has a 20-foot high ceiling. An earlier occupant had found the room so large he had partitioned it off into five rooms, but the removal of these partitions was one of the Duchess of York's priorities.

Over the years extra bedrooms and guest accommodation have been added to the house. An open-air swimming pool was built in 1938, and used before the war by the young Princesses. The air-raid shelters built behind the house are still intact.

Viewed from the wide lawn at the back, the house shows off the oriental arches, each with a crown at its pinnacle, that frame the five windows to the Saloon. From inside, the view over the terrace, with its tubs of trimmed box looking like sentinels, take the eye down to a wide glade flanked by magnificent cedar trees that were there

when George IV was planning his house.

The gardens give the Queen Mother the greatest pleasure because they are a lasting memorial to her husband. He created them out of a wilderness, enlisting the practical help of anyone who happened to be around at weekends and could be roped in to give a hand.

In the 1930s the Duke and Duchess of York spent almost every free week-end at Royal Lodge, in the early days taking picnic lunches with them because the house wasn't yet habitable. It was their retreat from the formal Court life in London, where they could indulge their love of the open-air, woodland walks, and the whisper of wind through tall trees.

Near the swimming pool is the two-storey miniature cottage, with cream-coloured walls and thatched roof, which was a gift to Princess Elizabeth from the people of Wales on her sixth birthday. Furnished throughout—it even has a bathroom with running water, something many full-size Welsh houses didn't have at the time—it stands only 15 feet high and is

a perfect place for children to play in.

Guests invited to Royal Lodge for Ascot week would remark afterwards that they had never seen a happier family than the Yorks. Breakfast was at 9, dinner at 8.30, and if the weather was fine everyone gathered in the sunken garden for tea after an afternoon at the races.

On Sundays the Royal Family worshipped, as they still do when they are staying at Windsor, in the little church built by George IV that stands just outside the garden hedges of Royal Lodge. Rambling roses trail along the fences that surround the Royal Chapel, two bells summon from the open belfry. It is a friendly little church, despite the rather ornate interior decoration of the chancel roof.

The Royal Family occupy a pew, sitting on green-covered chairs, that is not in view of the rest of the congregation. (The Duke of York, after he became King, had a nick cut in a pillar of the chancel arch so that by leaning forward, he could see who had turned up for Sunday service!)

Everything changed with the abdication;

Edward VIII and his three brothers congregated at Royal Lodge for the last time an hour before the King drove over to Windsor Castle to broadcast his famous abdication speech.

During World War II the King and Queen spent as many week-ends as they could at Royal Lodge, meeting up with their daughters who had been evacuated to Windsor Castle. These were the only occasions in five years when the King changed from his service uniform into "civvies".

But today, as she sits at her desk in the Octagon Room of Royal Lodge, and looks through the french windows and down the stone-flagged path bordering the herb garden, the Queen Mother must have mainly happy memories.

The house, halfway between Windsor Castle and Virginia Water, towards the eastern side of Windsor Great Park, lies not far from the public highway. But it is utterly private, the Queen Mother's very special home. Again, it is a home that one day might pass on to Prince Charles.

Top: *The comfortably-furnished Saloon, which overlooks the terrace*
Above: *A gentle and relaxed pose for a Cecil Beaton portrait taken in 1970*

Tulle, tiaras and tippets

It may seem unchivalrous, but it's probably true to say that when a waiting crowd of spectators, or an audience in a theatre, first see the Queen Mother step out of her Rolls Royce or appear in the Royal Box, the majority gasp with admiration at the magnificence of her dress and her sparkling jewellery, while a few lower their heads to whisper to companions: "What *is* she wearing today?" At least both groups speak with equal affection. At least the Queen Mother always looks like a Queen, albeit a cuddly Queen, and never like a president.

The truth is, the Queen Mother enjoys clothes. Fashion is a subject that interests her, more than it does either of her daughters, though she has never had any desire to "lead fashion". She likes to look regal—"never look down at your feet" was an early lesson from her mother—but she's just as happy throwing on an old coat, shoving a battered felt hat on her head, pushing her feet in gumboots, and setting off on a walk in the rain. She's not at all a vain lady. She's practical and believes in wearing the clothes that suit the occasion. And she has an excellent sense of colour.

It's interesting to reflect on the fact that the most impressionable years for the Queen Mother, when she was a teenager, coincided unhappily with World War I when materials for new dresses were in short supply, and talk of having nothing to wear was not considered very patriotic.

But then, of course, there came the wacky Twenties, when skirts displayed ankles and waistlines hovered around the hips. Lady Elizabeth Bowes-Lyon, as the Queen Mother then was, was a small, slim, dainty figure taking tea with friends in the afternoon then going perhaps to a dinner-dance in the evening wearing a loose, tasselled dress with her dark hair cut in a fringe.

She could be very elegant, too. When she opened a Sale of Work an observer noted: "She looked such a sweet-faced, pretty, gentle-natured girl as she appreciatively handled the lovely work and thanked the organisers. She wore a cafe-au-lait brown duvetyn skirt and loose Russian-shaped coat to match, a row of pearls around her lovely neck and a big black straw hat trimmed with soft black and gold ribbon."

After her marriage to the Duke of York her choice of what to wear changed, partly due to her new position, but partly because it pleased her to wear what her husband liked.

The Duke of York had a passion for detail, and strong likes and dislikes about women's *and* men's fashions. When the young King Peter of Yugoslavia came to call on him during the war wearing the uniform of the Yugoslav air force with a gold watch-chain threaded between the breast pockets, his host told him to take it off. "It looks damned silly and damned sloppy."

He would never have been as sharp with a lady, certainly not with his wife. But even so he usually made known his preferences. For instance, he did not like to see the Duchess of York in green. During the war it was said that another reason she did not wear this colour was because it was considered unlucky, but it's noticeable from photographs that the Queen Mother was not seen in green until some time after her husband's death.

Some 17 years before that event, in the autumn of 1935, a young luminary of haute couture, wrote proudly on the notepaper of his new address (26 Bruton Street, W1), to a lady whose betrothal to the Duke of Gloucester had just been announced. He was looking for work and asked if he might be permitted to submit ideas for her wedding dress. Lady Alice Montagu-Douglas-Scott, daughter of the seventh Duke of Buccleuch, replied from Drumlanrig Castle in ▶

1925 — 1936 — 1950

*Opposite—***Above:** *One of the earliest portraits of the ingénue Lady Elizabeth Bowes-Lyon in lavender silk.*
Below: *The young Duchess shows her love of hats as she moves to the neater, flapper look of 1926 from the Edwardian big-brimmed style*

Above: *The Queen Mother has always loved dramatic, often ornate fashion, and Mr. Hartnell, a rising young designer in the Thirties loved drama too. The black-and-white leaf print dress and jacket is an example of one of his earliest designs for her. The fur tippet was probably her own idea to keep off an August breeze! Right, 15 years later Norman Hartnell designed this swirling fringed dress for a plumper figure; the hat is unmistakably Hartnell, too*
Left: *History does not relate whether this was an over-enthusiastic bouquet, or a floral tribute to the "Lest We Forget Association" on a visit in 1924. Either way, the Queen Mother's office is often asked what she will be wearing in order to avoid a colour clash with a bouquet. They always explain that flowers of any colour will be appreciated*

Dumfriesshire, that she would call in to see him when she returned to London the following week. The name of the designer was Norman Hartnell. And, as a result of that letter, for the next 44 years, he was to be fashion designer to Queen Mary, Queen Elizabeth II, Princess Margaret and, of course, to Queen Elizabeth the Queen Mother.

Lady Alice asked Hartnell to make her wedding dress, and also the dresses of the eight bridesmaids who were to follow her down the aisle. Among them were Princess Elizabeth and Princess Margaret Rose, who were accompanied by their mother when they went to Bruton Street for their fittings.

In his autobiography, Silver and Gold, Norman Hartnell describes with the observant eye of an artist his first meeting with the Duchess of York. She "was in silver grey georgette, clouded with the palest grey fox, and her jewels were dew drop diamonds and aquamarines.

"The young Princesses, on each side of her, as she led them by the hand, wore little blue jackets, silver buttoned, and tiny grey hats wreathed in blue forget-me-nots, making a symphony of silver and blue.

"I thought it my duty to guide them at once through the rather crowded showroom to the privacy of a small room specially set apart for them in the rear of the building. But I noticed then, for the first time, the intentionally measured and deliberate pace of royal ladies. With lovely smile and gracious movement the Duchess of York acknowledged on either side the reverences of the women present and very slowly moved on and out of sight."

When King George VI was crowned, Hartnell was commissioned to design the dresses of the Maids of Honour—Madame Handley Seymour was given the honour of making the Queen's Coronation dress.

While Hartnell was on a visit to Buckingham Palace the King took him on a quick tour in order to show him paintings by Winterhalter, among them those of the Empress Eugénie of France and the beautiful Empress Elizabeth of Austria, who graced the European courts in the 19th century. In every case the ladies were

The world-renowned "Queen Mum" style emerges, first in Paris, where she amazed the chic socialites with fashion confidence.

More white organza for Ascot in the Fifties. The small toque hat balanced the very high heels. The longer skirts of the late Forties give way to the fashionably shorter lengths of the late Sixties. Coats are loose, dresses cross over the bodice and fabrics are soft silks and chiffons, always with a dramatic hat.

But it is in the evening, tiara-time, when the Queen Mother takes centre stage. Swathed in yellow silk taffeta (stole and bag to match), or gold-embroidered silk, or bead-encrusted organza, nestling in a white fox stole, with priceless heirlooms, she is what we want her to be—a Queen

wearing picturesque crinolines, or full-length, off the shoulder dresses with small waists. The elegance and grace appealed strongly to the King. Now, he suggested, if Mr. Hartnell could capture the same feelings in his designs.

Hartnell has often been given credit for the preference for crinoline ballgowns which the Queen Mother retains to this day, but when asked he was always ready to acknowledge the help of the King's keen eye.

A designer of royal apparel has to keep his wits about him, think ahead, and be prepared to make last minute changes. Buttons and button-holes on gloves must be big enough to make the gloves easy to put on and take off quickly. Zips should preferably not be used, in case they get stuck. Hats should be well off the face, so they do not hide it, and the use of veils discouraged. (The Queen Mother has only worn veils frequently in the last 10 years or so.) Shoes should not have very high heels—they can be precarious. (The Queen Mother, despite two serious falls, continues to ignore this advice even at 80!)

Royalty, there is no doubt, helps to set trends in fashion, and sometimes almost by accident. In June 1938, the Countess of Strathmore died, barely a week before her daughter was due to accompany the King on a state visit to France. Designs had already been approved and work almost completed on a glamorous wardrobe for five banquets, two state receptions, garden parties, and a gala visit to the opera.

The Queen could not possibly appear in bright colours so soon after her mother's death, but could she appear in chic Paris in midsummer in mourning black either? Hartnell had a quite brilliant suggestion: "Is not white a Royal prerogative for mourning, Your Majesty?" Purple was more usual, but there were precedents. It was agreed.

The visit had been put back three weeks in deference to the Queen, and in two weeks a whole wardrobe was created in white.

The Queen's appearance in Paris caused a sensation, particularly with the stunning white dress of cobweb lace and tulle ►

and the sweeping hat bordered with white osprey that she wore at Bagatelle.

When she sprung open a transparent lace parasol while watching a ballet, performed by the lakeside on the Ile Enchantée, she revived a fashion in a single moment.

World War I had precluded the Queen Mother from experimenting with teenage fashions as a girl, and World War II restrictions again governed fashion when she was in her forties. Early in 1940 the rag-trade was circulated with Ministry guidelines stipulating exactly how much material and work should go into a garment, even down to the number of seams and the width of the belt.

Queen Elizabeth could not be an exception and Hartnell was required to stick strictly to the rules. For some important soirées at foreign embassies, however, he felt the Queen must look impressive. So in place of forbidden embroideries he hand-painted wax-like lilac and glossy leaves on a gown of white satin. Fortunately the Queen was not restricted in the amount of jewellery she wore.

A talent to choose and match colours successfully has always been one of the Queen Mother's strengths where fashion is concerned. The same ability is apparent in the way she can plan a herbaceous border so perceptively. Clear, bright colours are usually the choice for all the ladies of the Royal Family, so that they stand out in a crowd. But during the war Queen Elizabeth deliberately chose to wear pastel shades—soft blues, greys and pinks—partly because they did not show up the all-pervading dust and dirt when she walked through bombed streets and partly because she thought it unfitting to wear "something frivolous". Her love of delicate shades and subtle blending has remained, but in hats especially she enjoys wearing creations that are not perhaps frivolous but are certainly feminine.

She has always been noted for her beautiful complexion and her striking blue eyes, and she does not believe in using heavy make-up which can show up lines. She prefers a light, creamy foundation and powder, giving a natural appearance, with a pale-rose

There are very few women—let alone of "a certain age"—who could get away with some of the Queen Mother's dramatic flourishes. An oblique band of fur, a hard-to-wear lime green, a suddenly shorter skirt . . . even a less than flattering outfit for Badminton Horse Trials in the rain!

rouge and a lipstick of a deeper tone. She has favoured the same hairstyle for many years now and though her hair is sometimes tinted, she is not afraid to show the silver that is naturally there.

Similarly, she does not believe in dieting—for any length of time at least—especially when she discovers she's forbidden the food she most enjoys. Her attitude has always seemed to be: I will do my best to please, but you must take me as I am.

In fact the Queen Mother is a couturier's dream—intelligently interested and happy to listen to suggestions, ultra-patient at fittings, erect in carriage and able to show off a designer's work to the best advantage. She refers to her clothes, especially the more grand affairs, as her "props". Norman Hartnell adored her. Until his death in 1979 he sent her a bouquet of red roses on her birthday, growing in number each year until he stopped at six dozen!

Today her clothes are still made by Hartnell's salon, but she no longer requires the number that she used to and, like the Queen, she has favourite dresses and coats that come out again and again. She will stick to a particular handbag for years, and she still owns an umbrella with a gold pencil fitted into the handle which she's had since her wedding.

From being a lovely young woman, good-natured and fun, the Queen Mother has matured into a beautiful old lady, gracious and stately. And if "clothes maketh a man" clothes have certainly helped make her a person loved by millions. "Just look what she's wearing! Doesn't she look absolutely fantastic!"

When the Queen Mother and the Norman Hartnell salon have decided on a fabric and design, a matching length is sent to Simone Mirman, or in recent years, Mr. Rudolf next door, to make up a hat. The Queen Mother nowadays loves veiling, she thinks it softens the face and is very feminine.

As with all fashion, some of the styles seem extreme in retrospect (that mélange of lemon feathers and tulle) but, whilst rarely in the vanguard of fashion, the Queen Mother's hats are always totally appropriate and flattering

On the course...

When the Royal Family talk amongst themselves, horses are the one subject they all know a great deal about. But from different standpoints. The Queen is an internationally recognised expert on flat-racing and the breeding of thoroughbreds. Prince Philip knows a great deal about the art of driving a four-in-hand. Princess Anne is a proven horsewoman of Olympic class, and Prince Charles, in one of his latest adventures, has taken up "jumping the sticks" with professional jockeys. Perhaps he was influenced by his grandmother, for she is not only an avid follower of steeple-chasing, but also one of the most knowledgeable and popular figures at any of the race-meetings she attends.

The Queen Mother loves going to the races, rain or shine. Often she will decide to attend at the last moment and, with only the police, the senior steward and the clerk of the course informed, will turn up unannounced. But the moment the crowd see

Left: *The traditional drive down the course at the start of Royal Ascot*
Inset: *With King George VI at Epsom*
Below left: *The expert comments*
Above: *The Queen and the Queen Mother study their race-cards. Prince Phillip has never been a keen race-goer,* *preferring the sport of four-in-hand*
Right: *Congratulating jockey David Nicholson after winning the Whitbread Gold Cup on Mill House at Sandown Park, 1967*
Below right: *With the Queen's racing manager and jockey, the Queen Mother and the Queen enjoy another victory*

the Queen Mother's standard raised on the flag-pole a great cheer invariably goes up from the punters, trainers and jockeys alike. They love having her among them as much as she enjoys being in their company. She doesn't bet and, over the years, though she's had some spectacular successes, she's had her disappointments, too.

If she cannot attend a race in which one of her horses is running she will turn on "the blower", giving news from the course, which has been installed in her dining room at Clarence House, and if the race is being broadcast, she will switch on the television. Racing, and steeplechasing in particular, is one of her very greatest delights.

The Queen Mother has always loved horses, and enjoyed watching thoroughbreds from King George VI's stables running in various Classics. But flat-racing was never to grip her as steeplechasing has. Indeed in the years immediately after World War II she was intrigued to see the enthusiasm that her eldest daughter was

now showing for the intricacies of "form".

It was at a dinner party at Windsor Castle in June 1949 that the Queen Mother's own enthusiasm was fired.

Among the guests was Lord Anthony Mildmay of Flete, the celebrated amateur National Hunt jockey whose character and racing record had already made him a legend. The previous March, riding Cromwell, he had charged into third place in the Grand National at Aintree, in spite of a cruel attack of cramp in the neck which meant he jumped the last fences with his head slumped to the side of the horse's neck.

Lord Mildmay could make the sport of steeplechasing sound exhilarating, and the Queen Mother was halfway to accepting his suggestion before he put it: why not buy a steeplechaser. The Queen Mother turned to her daughter. Princess Elizabeth nodded. She was all in favour—they would share a horse.

Peter Cazalet, who trained Mildmay's ▶

horses, searched around and lighted on just the right choice, both from the point of view of price and antecedents. Monaveen, the Irish-bred, nine-year-old half-brother of Cromwell, was purchased for £1,000, and the partnership of Queen Elizabeth and Princess Elizabeth was published in the Racing Calendar. The horse would be ridden under the Princess's new racing colours of purple with gold braid and scarlet sleeves, and black cap.

Wasting no time, Monaveen was entered for the early autumn meeting at Fontwell Park, West Sussex—the first horse to run for a Queen of England since Queen Anne won a race at Ascot in 1714. Princess Elizabeth went along to watch. Everyone hopes, but few really expect, a new owner to have a winner first time out. But Monaveen managed it (admittedly there were only three runners), romping home 15 lengths ahead of his nearest rival and earning the royal partnership £204 in prize money.

The horse went on to win at Sandown, then, on the last day of 1949, at 10–1, beat all the favourites at Hurst Park and collected £2,328 (over twice his purchase price) for his owners.

The following year, however, brought double tragedy. In May Lord Mildmay was drowned off the Devon coast when cramp struck during an early-morning swim, and in December Monaveen, attempting to repeat his victory at Hurst Park of the previous year, fell, broke a leg and had to be destroyed. The Queen Mother had flown down from Sandringham specially to see her horse run, and was very saddened.

By now she was racing under her own colours—buff-striped blue shirt with blue sleeves, black cap and gold tassel. She had bought a young French horse, Manicou, but her daughter, with her new baby, Princess Anne, occupying so much of her attention, had retired from the partnership.

The Queen Mother's racing colours are based on those of her grandfather, the 13th Earl of Strathmore (another ancestor, John Bowes, won the Derby no less than four times!), but when she saw them worn by her jockey for the first time she thought the blue was "not quite royal enough". In time she would have a new set where "the blue will be truly blue."

Gradually the Queen Mother added to her stable, buying cautiously and gaining in expertise all the time. Unlike some other owners she didn't employ a manager, but relied on her good friend and trainer Peter Cazalet.

By coincidence, after King George VI's death, the Queen Mother's fortunes on the course declined for two years because her two best horses were out of action. One of these, Devon Loch, was eventually to run one of the most extraordinary races in the history of the Grand National.

Devon Loch was bought for the Queen Mother as a five-year-old, with a condition that the previous owner would receive £1,000 on top of the purchase price if he ever won the Cheltenham Gold Cup and £2,000 if he won the Grand National—but

Above: *Seeking a second opinion from grandson Charles at Royal Ascot 1978*
Left: *Encouraging words for Charles before the start of his first steeplechase race at Sandown Park in March 1980. Riding Sea Swell, he came last but only four horses finished*

Left: *The tragic sequence showing Devon Loch's mysterious collapse during the 1956 Grand National*
Below left: *The Royal Family inspect the runners at Epsom for the 1962 Derby*
Below: *The Queen Mother with Double Star, one of her favourite horses, after winning the Novices' Chase at Sandown Park in 1957*

no more than £2,000 should he win both.

He had a few successful outings for a season or two, but by 1956 he was reckoned to be a good enough prospect to be entered for the National. He came third at Cheltenham, but this was only just over three miles and some still had doubts whether he could last over the four-and-a-half miles at Aintree. The betting put him at 100–7 in the race for the prize of nearly £9,000. The jockey was Dick Francis, who has gained even wider fame since then as the writer of racing thrillers.

The Queen Mother, the Queen and Princess Margaret were in the royal box, and as the gruelling race thundered on they became more and more excited as Devon Loch forged his way to the front. Four fences from home he was clear of Eagle Lodge, E.S.B., Gentle Moya and Ontray. Ontray fell at the last fence but one. But Royal Tan was rapidly making up ground on the leaders. However, Devon Loch cleared the final fence easily and up the long run-in to the finishing post he drew further and further ahead of the others.

Fifty yards from home Devon Loch was coasting. Then, without the slightest warning, his hindlegs slipped from under him, his forelegs crumpled, and his belly sank to the ground with his jockey helpless on top of him. It was the most ignominious and tragic end to the most famous steeplechase in the world, and to this day a mystery as to why it happened. An examination immediately afterwards showed the horse to be perfectly sound.

The Queen Mother commiserated with Dick Francis, then went down to see her horse. Patting him on the neck, she said: "You dear, poor old boy." Devon Loch ended his days grazing contentedly in the fields at Sandringham.

Over the years the Queen Mother has had her disappointments on the course, but she has never lost interest or thought of giving up. And she has had some remarkable successes. With horses such as Double Star, The Rip, Malkadar and Colonins she has notched up well over 300 winners. Even so she has not benefited financially as much as she might have, due largely to the fact that she doesn't think of selling off horses when they turn out to be duds or are past their

prime. Instead she finds friends who will give good homes to the failures, and she much prefers seeing the winners enjoying a well-deserved retirement. She likes visiting them, sugar lumps in her pocket and perhaps a basket of carrots in her hand. She always has a kind word for them.

Going to the races, especially to a steeplechase meeting, can be a bitterly cold experience, which is partly why so many people opt out nowadays and stay at home to watch the television coverage. But well into her late seventies the Queen Mother was prepared to brave the worst weather to see one of her horses running, to plough back and forth through the muddy grass to the paddock, wrapped up against the winds in practical if not exactly fashionable garb. She loves the atmosphere, and enjoys chatting to jockeys and trainers. And they in turn benefit from her knowledge—though she now owns few horses, she has lost none of her expertise.

If ever it came to going to the barricades to defend the Queen Mother you can safely bet the whole racing fraternity would be first in line. She's the favourite every time.

A portrait presented in 1971 to the Royal College of Music, of which the Queen Mother is President, painted by Leonard Boden

A Royal Duke returns

On May 28, 1972 the Duke of Windsor died at his house in Paris from cancer of the throat. He was 77. His body was flown to London, and then to St. George's Chapel, Windsor, where it lay in state.

Just over a week before, at the end of a state visit to France, the Queen had gone to visit her uncle, knowing that he was dying. It was, in part, a last attempt to heal a rift which dated back 35 years to the time when King George VI had created his brother Duke of Windsor and accorded him, but not his wife, the title of "Royal Highness". The Duke bitterly resented the Duchess being precluded from using the title. He swore he would never return officially to Britain until his beloved Wallis, for whom he had given up the Throne, was granted the same dignity as himself.

There is no authorised record yet available to the public to verify the feelings of the Queen Mother towards her brother-in-law at the time of the abdication, or subsequently. But it is generally believed that she felt lasting enmity about the heavy burden he placed on her husband's shoulders by his decision to step down from the Throne in order to marry Mrs. Simpson.

If this really was her feeling it was not shared by her husband apparently. For after the brothers met for the first time in nearly three years—at Buckingham Palace in September 1939—the King wrote in his diary: "We talked for about an hour. There were no recriminations on either side . . . I found him the same as I had always known him." The King and Queen had just returned from a tour of the London docks when the meeting took place, but the Queen was not present at it.

The King's sense of brotherly love was shown again on the very same day he underwent surgery to remove his left lung. He ordered three brace of grouse to be delivered to the London house where the Duke of Windsor was staying: "I understand he is fond of grouse."

However, notwithstanding his feelings towards his brother, the King did not receive the Duchess of Windsor at any time, and she did not attend the funeral of King George VI, nor that of his mother the following year. The Duke came on his own.

The present Queen Elizabeth has always shown compassion. She went to visit both the Duke and Duchess of Windsor when they came to London for an operation on his eye. She sent him a telegram on his 70th birthday. And in 1967, when a commemorative plaque to Queen Mary was unveiled in London, the Duke and Duchess rode in the official procession at the invitation of the Queen. Afterwards they were seen to talk briefly with the Queen Mother.

When her husband's body was brought

Top: *An uncrowned king comes home at last, to Windsor Castle in June 1972*
Above: *The unveiling of a plaque to Queen Mary in 1967—the first public recognition of the Duchess of Windsor by the Sovereign*

from France for burial, the Duchess of Windsor stayed at Buckingham Palace. The morning after her arrival she did not feel well enough to attend the Trooping the Colour ceremony, but drawing aside a curtain she watched the Queen set out for Horse Guards parade. That evening the Prince of Wales and Lord Mountbatten accompanied her when she asked to go to Windsor to see her husband's coffin lying-in-state.

The following day the interment took place privately in the royal burial ground at Frogmore within Windsor Great Park. In due time the Duchess of Windsor will lie there also, at her request and with the Queen's assent, at her husband's side.

Silver weddings

The Queen and Prince Philip celebrated their silver wedding anniversary in November 1972, and following the tradition set by the Queen's grandfather, George V, and carried on by his son, George VI, a special service of thanksgiving was held in London.

It was just over 24 years since the Queen Mother had joyously marked 25 years of marriage to King George VI. On that day—the bright sunny morning of April 26, 1948—they drove in an open landau, with Princess Margaret sitting opposite them, to St. Paul's Cathedral. In the early evening they toured 22 miles of London streets, acclaimed all the way.

Memories of that day must have come back to the Queen Mother as she knelt in Westminster Abbey, Prince Philip and the Queen at her side, to give thanks for the first 25 years of their married life.

Whether by design or by accident, speeches made by both the Queen Mother and the Queen on their silver wedding anniversaries laid emphasis on the value to marriage of a happy upbringing.

"The world of our day," said the wife of

George VI in 1948, "is longing to find the secret of community, and all married lives are, in a sense, communities in miniature. There must be many who feel as we do that the sanctities of married life are in some way the highest form of human fellowship, affording a rock-like foundation on which all the best in the life of the nation is built.

"Looking back over the last 25 years and to my own happy childhood, I realise more and more the wonderful sense of security and happiness which comes from a loved home."

In 1972, at a silver wedding celebration luncheon at Guildhall in London, the wife of Prince Philip began with a joke against those who mimicked her. "I think everybody really will concede that on this day of all days I should begin my speech with the words 'My husband and I'." She continued: "Now that we have reached this milestone in our lives we can see how immensely lucky we have been, or perhaps fortunate might be a better word.

"We had the good fortune to grow up in happy and united families. We have been fortunate in our children, and above all we are fortunate in being able to serve this great country and Commonwealth."

All the members of the Royal Family believe in the value of family life, and it is not just lip-service they pay. Others may think the nuclear unit, legal and blessed, is an outdated concept, but it is unlikely that even the youngest of the "Royals" will ever agree with them. Prince Charles, though admittedly no longer very young, regards the family unit as "the most important ▶

Opposite—**Top:** *Queen Elizabeth II and Prince Philip read messages of congratulations that poured in from all over the world on their silver wedding and (inset), nearly 24 years earlier, King George VI and his Consort celebrate the same landmark in their marriage* **Bottom:** *Setting out for the lunch at Guildhall from Buckingham Palace, 1972*

Above: *Following a royal tradition, a special service of thanksgiving was held at Westminster Abbey* **Left and right:** *Symbols of family unity in a country recovering from war, Elizabeth's parents attended a thanksgiving service on their anniversary at St. Paul's Cathedral*

aspect of our particular society", and he has paid tribute to "very wise and terribly sensible parents who have created a marvellous, secure, happy home" for him.

He would be the first to extend some of that credit to his grandmother and her ability to bring warmth and good humour to any gathering. Ever since he can remember, she has been a source of security, a person who gives enchantment to others by her own effervescence.

The Queen is in no doubt either. On her anniversary she expressed her views on marriage thus: "A marriage begins by joining man and wife together, but this relationship between two people, however deep at the time, needs to develop and mature with the passing years. For that it must be held firm in the web of the family relationships, between parents and children, between grandparents and grandchildren, between cousins, aunts and uncles.

"If I am asked today what I think about family life after 25 years of marriage I can answer with simplicity and conviction. I am for it."

The Queen Mother would agree with every word of that.

Opposite: *Three delightfully informal pictures of Queen Elizabeth and Prince Philip, which capture the warmth of a mature and happy marriage*

Above: *The whole Royal Family gathered in the White Drawing Room at Windsor for this silver wedding photograph by Patrick Lichfield*

Right: *Speaking at the celebratory luncheon at Guildhall in the City of London, November 1972*

A grand-daughter married

The Queen Mother was responsible for bringing Princess Anne and Mark Phillips together in the first place, though their paths had previously crossed briefly at the Eridge Horse Trials.

She had accepted an invitation to a cellar party in the City of London, in honour of the British equestrian team who had returned from the 1968 Mexico Olympic Games with a gold medal. To everyone's delight the Queen Mother took her grand-daughter along with her. "As a beginner at eventing, I was very overawed by the occasion," Anne said later.

Captain Phillips, then a lieutenant, was the youngest ever reserve rider with the team, and he was undoubtedly greatly attracted to the Princess. She was 18 and he was 20, just two months younger than Prince Charles. It hardly needs to be said that their great common interest was horses. But they were also drawn to each other as individuals.

In Mark's presence, Princess Anne became less bossy, less inclined to fly off the handle when something annoyed her. He in turn, could withstand the buffeting of any storm that did blow up. "I just love everything about her," he said after they became engaged.

Even though she is the Queen's only daughter, and sister to the heir to the Throne, Princess Anne has rarely been happy in accepting the publicity that automatically attaches to the position. This may be why the official announcement of her engagement did not come until some weeks after Captain Phillips had formally asked Prince Philip for the hand of his daughter. Prince Philip, it is said, broke the news to the family at a dinner party in honour of the 50th anniversary of the Queen Mother's wedding.

The wedding took place on another anniversary, November 14, Prince Charles' 25th birthday. There was just one bridesmaid—Lady Sarah Armstrong-Jones—and one page—her brother, Prince Edward. The bride's long veil was held in place by a tiara loaned by the Queen Mother and worn by the Queen at her wedding 26 years earlier.

The formal wedding group pictures taken at Buckingham Palace show an almost ecstatically happy mother and grandmother of the bride. Indeed, looking at them, almost seven years later, it seems hard to believe that the lady standing on the Queen's left was in her 73rd year.

The televised wedding in 1973 of the Queen Mother's eldest grand-daughter and Captain Mark Phillips was watched by hundreds of millions of people around the world. But the day still retained a family feeling, a case of the only daughter among four children leaving home to get married

Dogs...

History shows that the Royal Family's love of dogs goes back several generations. Queen Victoria so loved dogs—she owned 83 at the time of her death—she refused to have unwanted puppies destroyed, or their tails docked, and as patron of the Lost Dogs' Home at Battersea she was responsible for strays being kept for two days longer than the law required.

When his favourite Irish terrier died, Edward VII had some of its hair made into a bracelet. His wife, Queen Alexandra, kept so many pets at Buckingham Palace that her successor, Queen Mary, would not have a dog in the place—except for George V's Cairn terriers, first Snip, then Bob who took the King his morning paper.

Edward VIII was also very fond of Cairn terriers. He carried Slipper under his arm when he boarded the naval destroyer that took him into exile. Sadly the dog was killed by a snake not many months later.

The line of Royal corgis so much in evidence today dates back to 1933 when the Duke and Duchess of York bought their elder daughter a puppy and called him Dookie. He sired Crackers and Carol. Crackers was the Queen Mother's favourite pet for nearly 14 years. Before he died, in 1953, he was so lame he was pulled around

Whether by car, train or plane, the corgis accompany the Queen Mother whenever possible. In the centre—making friends with the mascot of the Irish Guards

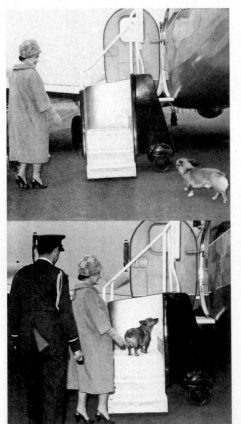

...and other interests

in a special type of miniature bath-chair.

The Queen Mother now has two corgis, Geordie and Blackie. Geordie it is safe to pat. Blackie is approached with great caution. In the past, it is recorded, royal corgis have bitten a Grenadier Guardsman, a policeman, a clock-winder, and a subaltern of the Irish Guards. Other incidents, no doubt, will come to light in time.

The Queen Mother is not a slave to her dogs. She is just very fond of them, and rarely so happy as when they accompany her on some brisk walk that would surely seem too fast for their short stubby legs.

Walking has always been one of the Queen Mother's favourite recreations. Another is Scottish country dancing—her graceful step and expert knowledge has both enchanted and bemused many a partner at the annual gillies' ball at Balmoral or the Christmas staff dance at Windsor. Age has never deterred her from taking to the floor nor the lateness of the hour sent her to her bed. But perhaps she does not dance quite so often as she once did, just as she does not wade into icy river waters, rod in hand, salmon in mind, quite so frequently.

The Queen Mother learned the art of fly-fishing as a young woman and over the years has become extremely proficient. Her enthusiasm has been passed on to Prince Charles, and now Prince Edward is also benefiting from Granny's experience on the salmon rivers of Scotland.

Right: *Trying a spot of trout fishing on Lake Wanaka during her 1966 New Zealand tour*
Below left: *The Queen Mother takes to the floor at the University of London President of the Union's ball*
Below right: *Attending Gun Dog Trials on the Balmoral estate in 1963*

Family weddings

A significant change in the pattern of royal weddings has taken place during the Queen Mother's lifetime. When she was a child, indeed up until the time of her own marriage, it was a tradition hardly ever broken that persons of royal blood married only those who were of their own kind. It was unheard of for a king to marry a commoner. Perhaps it still is. But certainly contrived marriages, even for princes, interlinking the Royal Houses of Europe, are a thing of the past. Even the heir to the Throne is expected to marry for love.

As one who herself had come from a warm family background, far removed from life at Court, the Queen Mother was delighted when the Duke of Kent announced his engagement to Katharine Worsley, the daughter of Sir William, Lord Lieutenant of the North Riding of Yorkshire. Their wedding at York Minster on June 8, 1961—the first royal wedding there since the marriage of Edward III in 1328—had all the joy of a truly family occasion.

Two years later the Duke's sister, Princess Alexandra, a particular favourite of the public and the Royal Family alike, was married in Westminster Abbey to the Honourable Angus Ogilvy, second son of the 12th Earl of Airlie whose castle home was a neighbour to Glamis. Once again tradition was broken, for Mr. Ogilvy declined the offer of a title that would make

Opposite—**Above:** *The Duke of Kent with his Yorkshire bride at Hovingham Hall, the Worsley family home*
Below: *The beautiful Princess Alexandra walks down the aisle at Westminster Abbey with her husband, the Hon. Angus Ogilvy*

Above: *A police umbrella for the Danish bride, Birgitte van Deurs, when she arrived at the tiny village church on July 8, 1972. The dismal weather didn't seem to dampen anyone's spirits for this simple country wedding*
Left: *The Queen Mother with the Duchess of Gloucester, the bridegroom's mother*
Below: *Cutting the cake at the reception, which was held at Barnwell Manor*

any children of the marriage other than plain Master and Miss. Another, less well-known, fact was that Mr. Ogilvy was not a member of the Church of England when he married in Westminster Abbey.

The least grand of all the royal weddings that the Queen Mother has attended was that of her nephew, Prince Richard of Gloucester, as he then was, to Birgitte van Deurs, the daughter of a Danish lawyer. She was a 20-year-old student at the Cambridge Language School when she met her future husband at a tea party—he was an undergraduate studying architecture.

The wedding took place in the tiny 13th-century village church near Barnwell Manor, the ancestral home of the Gloucester family in Northamptonshire, and was "a compromise between the traditional English wedding and the Danish one which is smaller, jollier, and more intimate," according to the bride. In keeping with the privacy that the bride and bridegroom preferred there were no photographs taken inside the church.

Sadly, less than two months after the wedding, Prince Richard's elder brother, the 30-year-old Prince William of Gloucester, was killed in a flying accident, and Prince Richard, who had always hoped for a life away from the limelight, inherited the duties and responsibilities of heir. His father, the 74-year-old Duke of Gloucester, died two years later.

A growing family

Like many grandparents, the Queen Mother must find it hard to believe at times that she has three fully-grown grandchildren, a great-grandson and many grand-nieces and grand-nephews who become more pretty or mature every time she sees them.

Lady Helen Windsor, the 16-year-old daughter of the Duke and Duchess of Kent, is going to be as beautiful as her mother—or her late grandmother on her father's side, Princess Marina, the memory of whom still makes old men sigh.

Lady Helen's brother, George, the Earl of St. Andrews, is showing every sign at 17 of being the most academically brilliant of all the Royal Family. At 12 he won a scholarship to Eton—the first "royal" ever to become a King's Scholar. There were 76 candidates competing for 15 scholarships and he gained eighth place. It was not only his parents who were proud of him that day.

The Queen Mother is not an intellectual. Her tastes could be described as middle-brow. So, though she's impressed and heartened by any of the family who do exceptionally well at school, she's not surprised or disappointed by those whose academic prowess turns out to be not much higher than average. "Try your very best, but don't break your heart over it," is the kind of advice she's most likely to give.

In Prince Charles the Queen Mother has an excellent example of a grandson who never found studying easy but who, none the less, earned sufficient marks to take a degree at Cambridge, a commission in the Royal Navy, and "wings" to fly almost anything from a helicopter to a jet fighter. When he strides into Clarence House with that jaunty walk of his, one hand fiddling with the signet ring on the little finger of the left hand, a smile on his face as broad as the Pentland Firth—the Prince of Wales must quite take his Granny's breath away. From the time of Queen Victoria, the Royal Family have all been small in stature—the men as well as the women—and it is only the present generation, following Prince Philip, who have risen to new heights.

Prince Charles' love for his grandmother is patently obvious. In practically every photograph taken of them together, she is either looking up to him, slightly appealing, slightly helpless—she has lost none of her ways of charming men even at 80—or he is smiling down at her, admiring, amazed even, at some shaft of wit or an insight into a contemporary situation that he might not expect her even to know about. They make one another laugh. They find it the easiest thing in the world to talk to each other non-stop. Invariably the Prince of Wales calls on ▶

*Opposite—**Above:** Prince Charles escorts his adored Granny back to Sandringham House after attending church service in 1969*
***Below:** A striking portrait of Princess Anne, aged 28, by Snowdon*
***Inset:** With the Queen Mother at Royal Ascot—Princess Anne shares her grandmother's love of hats*

***Top left:** Fellow spirits share a joke in Edinburgh. Both are wearing the robes of the Most Ancient and Most Noble Order of the Thistle*
***Top right:** On the steps of St. Paul's Cathedral, November 1979, at a service of dedication. Charles is wearing the uniform of the Parachute Regiment, of which he is Colonel-in-Chief*
***Above:** At the start of another Ascot meeting*
***Right:** With his favourite labrador, Harvey, at Balmoral. The picture was one of a series taken to mark the Prince's 30th birthday*

A familiar pose for the Queen Mother with all her young grandchildren—in this case Prince Andrew. She is always there to explain, to cheer up a rather bored young Prince and generally to make things more exciting. Over the years Andrew, mischievous as a child, has grown up to be a self-assured young man with a fierce competitive spirit and a love of adventure, which he shares with his elder brother, Charles. Like Charles, he has a very real love and respect for his grandmother

his grandmother practically the moment he returns from an overseas trip. She loves to hear all his news, to see how he's looking and make sure he's not overdoing things—which he very easily can.

It would be pointless to speculate on whether or not she chastens him for not being married yet—it's more than likely that she doesn't interfere at all—but she certainly keeps a close and loving eye on her grandson. (It is said that, on her advice, he shaved off the beard he sported briefly in public while he was in the Navy.)

Despite the fact that both the Queen Mother and Prince Charles have the wonderful ability to put even total strangers quickly at ease, despite the fact that the Prince of Wales is not averse to larking about a bit for the benefit of photographers, both grandmother and grandson are very much "private" people. They do not easily exchange confidences, even with their closest friends, and those who are in daily contact with the Queen Mother and Charles are often ignorant of their views on quite ordinary everyday topics. The Queen Mother especially likes to keep many of her thoughts and preferences strictly to herself.

Perhaps this is something she also has in common with Princess Anne who, while she has a reputation for being outspoken, is often only asking "to be left alone". An obvious difference between grandmother and grand-daughter is that while the Queen

Prince Edward is the Queen's youngest addition to the Royal "Firm" and has managed to grow up out of the limelight. Perhaps this is why he seems altogether quieter and more sensitive than his elder brothers and sister. He has his own special bond with Granny and in recent years, school permitting, he has accompanied her to several official functions, often with his cousins, Viscount Linley and Lady Sarah Armstrong-Jones

Mother obviously enjoys carrying out most if not all of her round of royal duties, Princess Anne appears at times to be bored. There is no doubt she does not possess the gracious manner of her grandmother—but then, who does?

From being a self-assured child, Princess Anne has grown into a courageous woman, strikingly beautiful in an evening gown, but more at ease in jeans and sweater, either riding a horse or talking about one. She gives the impression of being a straight-forward, no-nonsense young woman, and the Queen Mother would not disapprove of that, recognising as she must do, that a family would not be a family if everyone within it was the same. Princess Anne has a very deep affection and respect for her grandmother as the head of the Family. When the Queen and Prince Philip are on official duties abroad, the Queen Mother is the one person, apart from her husband, that she automatically turns to. Granny was there, at the end of the phone, when the Princess and Captain Phillips were held up at gun point in the Mall in March 1974. (The Queen and Prince Philip were in Indonesia at the time.) Granny was one of the very first to be informed of the birth of Master Peter, Princess Anne's first child and the Queen Mother's first great-grandchild.

One of the greatest delights for the Queen Mother is having a young family that spans ▶

in age from Prince Charles, 32 in November, to the Duke and Duchess of Gloucester's third child who was born in March 1980.

The extrovert personality and film star looks of 20-year-old Prince Andrew have really only made an impression on the public consciousness in the last two or three years. But the Queen Mother has naturally been in a position to follow his development closely since his birth on February 19, 1960 at Buckingham Palace—the first child, incidentally, to be born to a reigning monarch since Princess Beatrice, ninth and last child of Queen Victoria.

By all accounts Prince Andrew's exuberant character showed almost from the start. Once, when asked how old he was, he replied: "Three and a big bit." The Queen remarked at this stage in her second son's life: "I'm afraid that Andrew is no little ray of sunshine." His mischievous behaviour no doubt owed much to the seemingly inexhaustible reserves of energy which he still possesses. From being a rather tubby little boy he grew into a presentable teenager, but since leaving Gordonstoun, with two intervening terms at Lakefield College in Canada, he has shot up and slimmed down, so that now, a Royal Navy Midshipman training to be a pilot, he towers above the Queen Mother and even tops Prince Charles.

No-one, it is safe to say, will ever replace Prince Charles in the Queen Mother's affections, but she always appears equally proud in the company of either grandson. Both men make handsome escorts.

Prince Edward, by comparison, looks much less muscular than either of his brothers. One suspects he has not the same fierce competitive spirit of Andrew, nor the compulsion of Charles to prove himself in so many areas of sport and adventure. But he may prove to be more brainy than either of them in the end.

Three of 16-year-old Edward's closest friends are his cousins, Lady Sarah Armstrong-Jones and Viscount Linley, and James Ogilvy, Princess Alexandra's son. James, Lady Sarah and Prince Edward took early school classes together. Along with Lady Helen Windsor, the Duke and Duchess of Kent's daughter, all are almost the same age. At 18, Viscount Linley—or Dave Linley as he often introduces himself—is nearly three years older, just enough of an age difference to make him the unofficial leader of the group.

Even if he were not the eldest, it is difficult to see how Lord Linley's unconventional dress and outlook would not at least have some influence. Except on the most formal occasions he likes to wear his own individual variant of whatever is the current fashion among teenagers—always, it seems, with well-scuffed, unpolished cowboy boots.

Both Lord Linley and his sister attend Bedales (Lord Linley was due to leave July 1980), a private coeducational school near Petersfield in Hampshire where the informal atmosphere extends to the pupils

Viscount Linley and Lady Sarah Armstrong-Jones look on the Queen Mother's London residence as their second home and are often seen in the company of Granny. Lady Sarah has her mother's bubbly charm and Viscount Linley bears a strong resemblance to his father, Lord Snowdon, who has remained a good friend of the Queen Mother since his divorce from Princess Margaret

and teachers being on first name terms.

The Queen Mother has grown used to such modern ways. Indeed she likes to keep up with the latest trends, whether they be in education or pop music. She learns from "my young people", as she calls her teenage grandchildren, and they in turn find her marvellously tolerant of their ideas. They don't think of her as being "old" at all!

They like to bring her presents they have made themselves—a well-designed and executed piece of wood furniture from David Linley, a piece of pottery from Andrew when he was at Gordonstoun.

Lady Helen Windsor is already an accomplished pianist, and Lady Sarah Armstrong-Jones, who has much of the easy friendly manner of her grandmother, is developing the familial knack of mimicry.

James Ogilvy, just over a week older than Prince Edward, has the same nervous energy as his father. He is an enthusiast, and his enthusiasm for one particular sport or interest changes almost weekly.

The Ogilvy children, James and his 13-year-old sister Marina, hold a special place in the Queen Mother's affections because their father is the second son of the 12th Earl and Countess of Airlie. Both parents are now dead, but Princess Alexandra's marriage in 1963 meant that the Queen Mother's family, the Strathmores, and their neighbours in Scotland, the Airlies, were joined in marriage after centuries of friendship and service to the Crown.

The Queen Mother herself is the last surviving child of the 10 children of the 14th Earl of Strathmore who grew up all those years ago at Glamis Castle and St. Paul's Walden Bury at the start of the

century. David Bowes-Lyon, her favourite younger brother died from a heart attack in September 1961.

The Queen Mother very rarely returns to Glamis Castle, scene of so many of her own childhood memories, but she loves to welcome her grandchildren to spend summer days at Birkhall—for today's Royal Family the house of pleasant memories.

It is great consolation to her that she has such a fine family of young folk gathered around her. All different in character, all leading lives that are exciting in their various ways. And if she is glad to have them, they are certainly delighted to have her. There can be few better grannies.

Above left: *Celebrating her 75th birthday at Royal Lodge. The Queen Mother is holding a present from Prince Andrew—two pottery dishes he made himself at school*
Above right: *Lady Helen Windsor—a portrait taken by her father, the Duke of Kent, shortly before her confirmation at Windsor Castle in 1978*
Below: *At the christening of one of the newest members of the ever-growing Royal Family—Lord Frederick Windsor, son of Prince and Princess Michael of Kent, who was born on April 6, 1979*

Clarence House

Above: *Relaxing with a book in her private sitting room*
Right: *The main gateway to Clarence House, on the right, in Stable Yard*
Below left: *In front of her London home on her 60th birthday*
Below right: *The working Queen Mother at her desk, which overlooks the garden*

Central London, it has often been said, is really a series of villages, all running into one another. If that is the case then the "royal village"—Great Royalty it might be called—runs east from Kensington High Street, to Hyde Park Corner, south to Buckingham Palace, and east again to Clarence House, St. James's Palace and York House.

Princess Margaret, the Countess of Athlone and the Duke and Duchess of Gloucester live at the Kensington Palace end. The Duke and Duchess of Kent live at York House, butting on to St. James's Palace. And since May 1953, Clarence House has been the official home of Queen Elizabeth the Queen Mother. She resides there from early February until August, and from October till Christmas.

It is a beautiful hotchpotch of a building, being two back-to-back houses joined into one. The front, creamy-white and handsome, faces across lawns on to the Mall. The rear, in Ambassador's Court, is unadorned brick and looks much older and less grand. The Queen Mother can come out of the back door of Clarence House—known really as the Household door—cross the courtyard of about 100 feet or so, and call on the Kents. Conversely, the Duke and Duchess of Kent's children can pop over to visit their great-aunt—something she likes them to do.

Buckingham Palace is literally just up the road, and from upstairs one can look across to Hyde Park Corner and to where the Queen Mother's home after her marriage, 145 Piccadilly, used to stand before the area

was demolished to make way for traffic.

Clarence House itself was built in 1825 by John Nash for the Duke of Clarence, who had lived in a small house on the same site since 1790. When he became William IV in 1830 he continued to use it as a home, linked as it was by a corridor to the state rooms of St. James's Palace next door.

Later the Duchess of Kent, Queen Victoria's mother, occupied the house for over 20 years. Others who lived there for lengthy periods were Alfred, Duke of Edinburgh, Victoria's second son, and the Duke of Connaught, her third son. He lived at Clarence House until his death in 1942.

For the remaining years of World War II the house became the headquarters of the Red Cross and the St. John Ambulance Association and Brigade.

From 1949 Princess Elizabeth and Prince Philip made it their home—Princess Anne

was born there—and it might have remained so for many more years than it did, had it not been for the untimely death of King George VI. On the Queen's accession, the Queen Mother and Princess Margaret left Buckingham Palace and moved down the road to a house which was at least in much better condition than it had been for many years. Prince Philip had supervised considerable modernisation. When he first saw the house several of the rooms were still lit by gas, and bathrooms were almost non-existent.

Today, after 27 years of living in Clarence House, the Queen Mother has got the place pretty much as she likes it. And the house certainly exudes the warmth and graciousness of her personality to any visitor who steps inside. It has a feeling of being lived in, and cared for. There is a silence measured only by the slow tick-tock

of gleaming brass pendulums, interrupted occasionally by the throaty cough of a septuagenarian courtier in another room. The Queen Mother has a fine body of spritely gentlemen around her, one or two of whom are fairly elderly and who shout into telephones and stand most erect when sipping an aperitif.

Huge bowls of flowers and jardinières spilling fuchsias give fragrance and fresh colour to the rooms and corridors which, in the main, are decorated in pearl-grey and white.

Little remains of Nash's original work, except the ceilings and gleaming mahogany doors, but all around, in paintings and photographs are memories of a family life going back centuries—George III in Garter robes, painted by Allan Ramsay; Simon Elwes' painting of King George VI investing Princess Elizabeth with the Order of the ▶

Garter. There are other modern artists' work represented too—Augustus John, Lowry, Sickert, John Piper and Edward Seago.

On either side of the fireplace in the Queen Mother's morning room are glass-fronted cabinets displaying her magnificent collection of Red Anchor period Chelsea china that has been collected over many years.

The Queen Mother still studies auction catalogues carefully, and if she finds something she thinks might be interesting, one of her Household visits the sale-room. If his report is favourable, then a bid will be put in. The Queen Mother is especially attracted by an antique or painting that has some connection with her own family. And she has a particular penchant for Regency wine coasters.

When any of her racing friends come to lunch she may have one of her racing cups—perhaps the cup won by Manicou on Boxing Day 1950—displayed on the table. (Before other, non-racing visitors arrive, she has been known to cover up her copies of Sporting Life and the Racing Calendar with The Times and Financial Times.)

The Queen Mother enjoys reading—preferably something light—and likes to sit with a book in the drawing room when the sun is pouring through the windows. Or perhaps she will "play a little something" on the grand piano. Over the years many happy hours have been spent by the Queen Mother and her children, particularly Princess Margaret, round the piano singing songs from hit musicals or lilting Scottish ballads.

Beyond the drawing room at Clarence House is the Queen Mother's private sitting room with its George II marble mantel-piece, a collection of miniature furniture, a painting of Queen Elizabeth in her Coronation robes, and another of the young Princess Elizabeth in a blue dress, painted by Moynihan.

In a corner of the sitting room, next to a window, is the Queen Mother's "working desk". Even though it is fairly large, its top is scarcely visible beneath the blotter, the china basket that holds a dozen or more pencils and pens, the floral glass paper-weight, and the stockade of framed photographs and miniature paintings of her family that surround the edges of the desk,

Opposite: *Looking out from the terrace above the main entrance of the house*
Above: *The drawing room in 1949, when Clarence House was the home of our present Queen*
Below: *At a summer party, and the corgis are not left out*

pushing out the ivory-coloured telephone to a separate side table.

Directly facing the Queen Mother as she sits at her desk—by habit placing her handbag behind her and not on the floor—is what looks like a miniature firescreen. Made of gilt with three crystal glass panels, it was executed by Laurence Whistler for a former Private Secretary, Major Harvey, to give to the Queen Mother as a farewell present when he retired.

The centre panel neatly holds a sheet of Clarence House notepaper, renewed each morning with a typed list of the Queen Mother's engagements for that day.

The other two panels carry engravings depicting on the one side "Duties", and on the other "Pleasures". The "Duties" incorporate a montage of a microphone, trowel, drums, scissors, mortar-board and key—symbols of the round of public duties that members of the Royal Family perform. Beneath is an engraving of a limousine

leaving the gates of Buckingham Palace.

On the "Pleasures" side are binoculars, musical instruments, a net to land salmon and the mask of Terpsichore, the muse of dancing. The scene at the foot of the panel shows an open landau progressing up the course at Ascot. The whole comprises a novel and useful piece of art.

Clarence House is primarily a private home, but occasionally it is used, like Buckingham Palace, for formal matters of state.

When the Queen is abroad, three or four senior members of the Royal Family are appointed Councillors of State, and any two of them in consort can exercise many of the powers of the Sovereign, including the signing of Acts of Parliament, but excluding the awarding of honours.

Privy Councils are held at Clarence House when the Queen Mother is acting as Councillor of State. Privy Councillors congregate in the library and wait for a bell

to ring, whereupon they file into the morning room where the Queen Mother, along with another of the Councillors of State, receives them and presides over business. All the members, by tradition, remain standing throughout the meeting.

In delightful contrast to these formal occasions, the Queen Mother will sometimes invite one or two Councillors to stay on for lunch, and in the summer—even on what others might consider a decidedly coolish day—a table will be spread in the garden. She is not a heavy eater, but like anyone has her preferences—she finds a piece of Caithness cheese rounds off a meal nicely.

The Queen Mother, like the Queen, enjoys eating out-of-doors. And she rarely seems to feel the cold, just as her daughter the Queen, can wear a woollen suit in temperatures over 70°F without showing the slighest concern. It must be something in the Royal blood!

First great-grandchild

Sitting happily on his mother's lap, nine-months-old Master Peter rather steals the show on Princess Anne's 28th birthday

Above: *The Queen Mother's first great-grandson was christened at Buckingham Palace on December 22, 1977*
Right: *These pictures were taken at Balmoral in 1979 to mark the 32nd wedding anniversary of the Queen and Prince Philip. Two-year-old Peter made sure that they will be among the happiest pictures in the Royal Family album*

Towards the end of the Queen's triumphant Silver Jubilee year, Princess Anne gave birth to her first child—a son—on November 15. Not surprisingly, when asked for her reaction to the news of her first great-grandchild, the Queen Mother said: "This is one of the happiest days of my life."

Peter Mark Andrew Phillips was christened in traditional fashion in the music room at Buckingham Palace. The Prince of Wales was among the five godparents, and the oldest person present was the 94-year-old Princess Alice, Countess of Athlone, the only surviving grandchild of Queen Victoria and the baby's great-great-great-aunt.

Master Peter Phillips is the first grandchild of a ruling sovereign for five centuries to be born a commoner. Since 1917 a grandchild of the monarch does not automatically have a title at birth. Normally a hereditary title is given to the father, as happened with Lord Snowdon, but not in the case of the Honourable Angus Ogilvy, who declined a title when he married Princess Alexandra. In precedence to Princess Margaret and her children, young Peter Phillips, plain Master or not, is fifth in line to the Throne—a commoner among princes and very much a "Royal".

Joy and jubilation

The picture on the left, taken at the wedding of Princess Anne sums up very well the relationship between the Queen and the Queen Mother. Today the Queen has been on the throne for 28 years—three years longer already than her grandfather King George V. The Queen Mother has been a widow now for some 28 years. The picture is of two mature women, both looking younger than their years and each revealing in their expressions strong feelings of mutual love and contentment.

It is comparatively rare these days for the Queen and her mother to be photographed together. In processions they ride in separate coaches—the Queen Mother very often escorted by Prince Andrew and Prince Edward. The Queen's own heavy list of engagements means they may go days or even weeks without seeing each other. But they talk almost every day on the phone. The easy relationship between mother and daughter has not diminished over the years, though in public, ever since her daughter came to the Throne, the Queen Mother has been careful to remain in the background.

During the Queen's Silver Jubilee year of 1977 the Queen Mother played the role expected of her at official ceremonies and celebrations. But what private joy and jubilation she must have felt at seeing how the nation and the Commonwealth responded to 25 years' reign by her daughter. Any doubt about the popularity or even the survival of the monarchy was swept aside by the great torrent of rejoicing.

King George V, on returning to Buckingham Palace after a tour of London's East End during his Silver Jubilee in 1935, expressed genuine surprise at the crowd's overwhelmingly enthusiastic welcome. "I am beginning to think they must really like me for myself," he remarked. The Queen, as she walked through the streets after the service of thanksgiving at St. Paul's Cathedral in June 1977, must have experienced a similar reaction.

Those close to her often remark that the Jubilee year boosted the Queen's self-confidence and gave her a fresh awareness of the influence of the monarchy, especially in Commonwealth affairs, which made the idea of abdication in favour of Prince Charles at some point in the future appear even less of a possibility than before.

Great and far-reaching social and political changes have taken place in the world since the Queen came to the Throne, and perhaps she has been better suited than her mother to accept and adjust to some of them. The Queen Mother remembers with deep affection the thousands of men and women who, while the Queen was still a child, gave service to the King in the colonies of the ▶

Above right: *Not since the Queen's Coronation in 1953 had there been such a display of enthusiastic loyalty and national pride as during the Silver Jubilee year*
Right: *Riding in the State Coach to the thanksgiving service at St. Paul's Cathedral on Jubilee Day 1977*

Empire. And she would probably be the first to admit that she belongs to an older generation who still think on these things.

The Queen, for her part, would surely acknowledge the debt she owes her mother. At the Jubilee thanksgiving service in 1977, the then Archbishop of Canterbury, Dr. Donald Coggan, said: "King George VI and his beloved Queen in days of war and of post-war stress taught us afresh what duty means. The years that followed that reign have not been easy, but the foundation then laid has proved strong enough for another sovereign to build upon, and this she has done."

On the same day the Lord Mayor of London spoke more simply of the Queen being "blessed with a mother whose special place in the hearts of the people has seldom, if ever, been equalled in our long history."

The Queen Mother is extremely proud of what her daughter has achieved during her reign so far. She knows, too, that the late King would have been just as proud. And that, in the end, is probably what gives her most joy of all.

Right: *Mother and daughter regularly attend the Badminton Horse Trials*
Below: *A touching moment as the Queen Mother pins a sprig of shamrock to her daughter's coat on St. Patrick's Day, 1980*

An exceptionally charming study for a group portrait by Michael Noakes, completed in 1979

Lifetime of service

Nowadays, the Queen Mother takes life a little more slowly than she did, say, five years ago—it would be surprising if she did not. But even at 80 she can still fulfil a day of engagements and be much less weary than some half her age. If anything she seems to become livelier as the day moves on. And yet, paradoxically, she has always maintained she is basically indolent. At one time she kept a notice on her desk which read "DO IT NOW"—though she never believed it had the slightest effect.

The truth is, the Queen Mother is not one of the hurriers of this world. Like Prince Charles, she is not renowned for her speed in clearing a desk of papers. She does not always arrive for appointments on time, but such is her genuine interest in people she

often upsets carefully pre-arranged time-tables by lingering longer than planned. She tells whichever aide is accompanying her to tap his foot as a sign if he thinks she really ought to move on.

For nigh on 57 years—ever since her marriage—Queen Elizabeth the Queen Mother has been "moving on", meeting tens of thousands of people, making speeches, laying foundation stones, launching ships, inspecting troops, attending banquets, touring cities, walking mile upon mile. And not once has she appeared bored, hardly ever irritable, never unsmiling. Always the gracious wave, the friendly word, the caring interest. She is not lazy! The truth is rather to be found in the maxim she sometimes quotes to others: "Your work is the rent you pay for the room you

occupy on earth." And in the reply she once gave to a question posed by the biographer Dorothy Laird: "If one loves one's country—as one does—such service is something one is proud to do and to give." The words may sound slightly pompous, even old-fashioned, but for the Queen Mother the sentiment is as real as the lady herself.

In the financial year beginning April 1980 the Queen Mother is entitled to receive £244,00 from the Consolidated Fund—the provision voted by Parliament, and inflation-linked, that is made annually to members of the Queen's family. Prince Philip receives £135,000, Princess Anne £85,000, and Princess Margaret £82,000. Prince Charles receives nothing from the Consolidated Fund, deriving his main

Left: *King George VI and Queen Elizabeth approaching St. George's Chapel, Windsor, for the annual Garter service*
Right: *As Duchess of York, at the centenary celebrations of the Stockton-Darlington Railway in 1925*
Below left: *Signing the visitors' book at the Festival of Britain, which was declared open by King George VI from the steps of St. Paul's Cathedral in 1951*
Below right: *An ex-Serviceman warms to the young Duchess—a slender figure with a captivating manner*

income from the Duchy of Cornwall. The Queen's entitlement from the Civil List is £2,716,300.

Some argue that the allocations made to the Royal Family are excessive, even though a very large part goes on paying staff and official entertaining. Others stoutly believe that the role of the monarchy in present-day society is worth preserving at almost any cost.

What seems certain is that, even if people were paying out twice the amount they are, they would still turn out in their thousands to cheer the Queen Mother. And she, it is almost as certain, would carry out what she regards as her pleasure and her duty, provided the people still wished it, even if Parliament were drastically to reduce her allowance. Shortly after her husband died

she used these words: "My only wish now is that I may be allowed to continue the work that we sought to do together." Her attitude has not altered.

Even when she reached her 80th year—20 years past the retirement age of others—the Queen Mother was still carrying out an average of nearly three engagements a week. Several times she has been advised to shed some of her responsibilities. And each time she has agreed to do so. But when her Private Secretary has come to her with a list of annual visits she might perhaps discontinue, the Queen Mother's protest has always been: "But I can't give *those* up. I so love going. You must find something else."

Fatigue, like sex, was something the Queen Mother's generation grew up never admitting. Even so, the Queen Mother has

always been blessed with extraordinary stamina. Well into her seventies, she could stay up far into the night to dance a Dashing White Sergeant or an Eightsome Reel. Her only major health worries came in the Sixties, with an appendectomy in 1964 and a major abdominal operation shortly before Christmas two years later. When she cracked a bone in her left foot she insisted on keeping an appointment to launch a liner in Newcastle-upon-Tyne. She allowed herself to be pushed along in a wheelchair, but when she realised she was not visible to those at the back of the crowd, she insisted on standing up and walking the rest of the way.

By general consent, no-one in the Royal Family has a better "crowdside manner" than the Queen Mother. She makes every ▶

Left: *Visits to schools appear frequently in the Queen Mother's diary and are always thoroughly enjoyed by everyone. Here she looks at what the children have made at Moor House School, Surrey, in 1953*
Centre: *About to make her first flight with the Duke of York in 1935 on the way to a Brussels exhibition*
Below left: *Receiving a gift for Prince Charles at Eldoret on her second visit to Uganda in 1959*
Below right: *Arriving at Chelsea Barracks, London, to inspect the 1st Battalion Irish Guards in 1928*
Right: *The Queen Mother has always taken an active and informed interest in the arts. Opera and ballet are particular favourites and whenever possible she attends the Gala Performances at the Royal Opera House, Covent Garden*

person within smiling distance feel she is looking directly at them. No-one who has spoken with the Queen Mother has ever felt her attention wandering. Press photographers love her for the umpteen chances she gives them to get their picture. Children, rehearsed to distraction to curtsy or bow when presenting a bouquet, find their fears banished when the moment finally arrives and the Queen Mother bends down to have a word, the *right* word, with them. Only those local dignitaries who are officious suffer her crushing disregard. Like the Queen, the Queen Mother is capable of showing her displeasure with one deadly-aimed stony stare. When she suspects that the front line of a welcoming party has been carefully preselected, she is quite likely to break ranks in order to have a word with those unfavoured at the back. Very little escapes her eye, or ear.

A widow once wished Her Majesty many happy returns for her birthday, even though it was still some way off. The Queen Mother was curious as to why the lady was so clear about the date. "Simple, Ma'am," came the reply, "it's my birthday too." Nothing more was said, but on August 4 a greetings telegram from the Queen Mother was delivered to the widow's address.

In very recent years, despite her reluctance to "slow down", efforts have been made to select official engagements that will place as little physical strain as possible on the Queen Mother. When possible the number has been reduced to one or two in a day, instead of three or four, with travelling cut to a minimum. But while the Queen and Prince Philip, and Prince Charles, now undertake most of the long overseas tours, it sometimes goes unremembered that the precedent for these was set by the Queen Mother, when she was the wife of the Duke of York.

In 1927, the Duke and Duchess of York travelled 30,000 miles on a tour to Australia and New Zealand that lasted six months. But for the war she and King George VI would have made several overseas tours. As it was, his illness precluded the Commonwealth tour they would have made in 1949, which was eventually begun by their daughter, Princess Elizabeth, and Prince Philip only five days before the King's sudden death in 1952.

The Queen Mother has always enjoyed going abroad, and interestingly she has

travelled far more widely in the 28 years of her widowhood than in the 29 years that she was married. Since 1953, when she visited what was then Southern Rhodesia, she has paid official or semi-official visits overseas almost every year. She has been to France six times, Australia and New Zealand twice, and Canada no fewer than seven times—most recently at the age of 78.

Unlike the Queen and Prince Charles, the Queen Mother never feels the least bit queasy at sea, and flying perturbs her not at all. She made her first flight as long ago as 1935—from London to Brussels. Prince Philip was the first member of the Royal Family to fly in a jet aircraft—Comet 1—but the Queen Mother, always ready for a new adventure, followed his example only two weeks later. When she landed back in

England after a four-hour flight over France she immediately sent a telegram to the 600 (City of London) Squadron of which she was Honorary Air Commodore: "I am delighted to tell you that today I took over as first pilot of a Comet aircraft . . . What the passengers thought I really would not like to say."

Long flights do not bore her as they do others—when she travels by scheduled airline she will sometimes go aft to talk with other passengers. In 1958 she set up a new record by flying 25,800 miles round the world, the first Queen in history to do so. Nowadays, like all the Royal Family, she makes good use of helicopters to save time and to allow her to cover several engagements in a day. Here again she was among the first to recognise the value—her first

helicopter flight was made in April 1956.

A journalist once wrote that the Queen Mother made laying foundation stones appear to be one of the most pleasant ways of spending an afternoon. It was an apt description of her approach to the many somewhat uninspiring roles that royalty are constantly asked to undertake. But what the writer omitted to note was the inspiring effect simply of the presence of the Queen Mother. It was most noticeable in wartime, but in peacetime, too, factory managers have reported an increase in production immediately following a visit. She has an almost uncanny way of giving people a fillip.

Speeches from the lips of royalty on such visits have a reputation of containing more bromides than bons mots. And no doubt the ▶

Above, left and right: *The Queen Mother always receives a tremendous welcome when she visits one of her regiments—in this case, the Black Watch (left) and the 9th/12th Royal Lancers (right)*
Left: *In her role as Chancellor of London University on Presentation Day. In the 25 years that she has held this office, the Queen Mother has brought her characteristic enthusiasm to all sorts of university occasions*

Queen Mother has been handed her share of platitudes to read out at banquets and in town halls. However, when a suitable opportunity does arise, she is prepared to expound very clearly her firmly-held views on such topics as the virtues of family life, the erosion of individual freedom, and the importance of integrity. The light, bell-like tones of her voice may not give Churchillian weight to her words, but the underlying message contained in many of her speeches would no doubt make the old statesman, were he still alive, lift his head in admiration.

For instance, to an audience at the Albert Hall, the Queen Mother declared: "We must oppose with all our might any attempt to belittle the sacrifices of the last war or to lament them as purposeless. Those who laid

down their lives did not ask for conditions and guarantees. They offered everything and expected nothing. Have we who have survived offered too little and expected too much?"

She warned the citizens of London when she received the City's Freedom: "Only ordered freedom is true freedom. Nothing stands out more clearly amid the discords and conflicts of our age than the danger of the misuse of language which preaches licence in the name of liberty, or uses the phrases of democracy as a cloak for the most cruel tyranny."

And this was the message she once gave to the young people of South Africa: "First, in these days when freedom is greatly curtailed, and regulation is almost universal, do not lose your own individuality; it is your

most precious possession; and next, never be content with what is mediocre and ugly. You may sometimes have to accept it, but never be content with it."

The Queen Mother is by no means just a kindly face under a feathery hat. A woman of deep faith, with strongly-held—some would say reactionary—views on many of the changes in society that have come about in her lifetime, she holds firmly to the moral standards taught her as a child and deeply regrets that many apparently think some of these concepts less important than they were. Several of the organisations of which the Queen Mother is patron are to do with children or young people and she welcomes this contact with the future, though again she rarely misses an opportunity to point out what she sees as dangers. The training ▶

Far left, top and bottom: *The world of light entertainment has not been without its share of attention. The Queen Mother has attended nearly every Royal Variety Performance since the 1950s*
Far left, centre: *Holding the traditional nosegay, the Queen Mother leaves Westminster Abbey after the Royal Maundy service and distribution of alms in 1970*
Above: *Whatever the occasion, whatever the age group, the Queen Mother has a marvellous knack of putting people at ease. From soothing the tears of disappointment at a curtsy that has gone disastrously wrong to bringing genuine interest to any function, no matter how dull, she has the ability always to hit the right note*

Above left: *A picture of regal splendour, the Queen Mother attends a Gala Performance at the Royal Opera House in Spring 1980*
Above right: *Showing a certain expertise on a visit to a new youth club in the East End of London early in 1980*
Left: *Away from all the duty and decorum, the Queen Mother enjoys a brisk walk in crisp winter sunshine, her corgis ever trotting after her*

of body, mind and character are more precious, she once told a Cambridge audience, than "the breathless pursuit of technical mastery."

An astonishing total of over 300 organisations benefit from the Queen Mother's support and patronage, ranging from the Royal School of Needlework to the Keep Britain Tidy Group. Somehow she manages to keep in touch with all of them. She holds honorary degrees from universities as far apart as Dalhousie in Nova Scotia to Auckland, New Zealand.

Since 1955 she has been Chancellor of London University—an office which holds for her much more than a merely token interest. Twice a year she presides over the Presentations, patiently "nodding through" some 2,000 new graduates. At student dances she happily takes the floor with long-haired, and most probably republican-minded, young men who have been known to be less than proficient in executing a waltz. "Don't worry," she smiled sweetly to one President of the Students' Union as he stumbled round the floor, "you haven't knocked my tiara off—yet."

The Queen Mother's sense of fun is well known to the many army regiments of which she is Colonel-in-Chief and to all the Women's Services of which she is Commandant-in-Chief. Attendance at a regimental dinner where the Queen Mother is the guest of honour guarantees a lively evening.

Indeed it is hard to imagine an occasion—be it formal banquet or family gathering—where the Queen Mother's presence does not add zest, enchantment and a feeling of infinite security.

By the time the Queen Mother reached her 50th birthday she had proved herself the most successful Queen Consort in history. She had sustained a King and inspired a country through royal abdication and wartime blitz. She had always been regal, but at the same time *real*, blessed with the ability to draw others to her.

The Times summed up her character thus: "She speaks to all men and women on the level of common experience. . . . She is never afraid to challenge the over-sophisticated . . . she ignores the cynics and the pessimists and holds up for admiration the things that are lovely and of good report."

At 80, she hasn't changed.

Lord Mountbatten

The Queen was on holiday at Balmoral when on August 27, 1979 radio programmes were interrupted with the horrifying news of the murder of 79-year-old Lord Mountbatten, his 14-year-old grandson, Nicholas, and a teenage friend. One of the Queen's first actions, deeply shocked though she was, was to drive over to Birkhall to comfort her mother, or to break the news if the Queen Mother had not already heard.

Lord Mountbatten was of the Queen Mother's generation, and one of the most eminent of her contemporaries. Though he had faced mortal danger on several occasions during his long life, the manner of his death—the cruel madness of it—deeply shocked the Queen Mother as it did the world. She and he had witnessed in their lifetimes the assassinations of many of the crowned heads of Europe. But that anyone so close to the British Royal Family should be so threatened . . .

The Queen Mother is the matriarch of the Royal Family. Lord Mountbatten was like a grandfather—certainly to Prince Charles who adored him. The wreath placed in Charles' name at the funeral in Romsey Abbey carried the message: "To my HGF and GU . . ."—to my Honorary Grandfather and Great Uncle.

Lord Mountbatten had planned his own funeral like a complicated naval operation. He used to tell people about it, then invite them to come along. He was a salty, energetic character, who, incidentally, had a more intimate knowledge of the intricate ancestry of the Royal Family than anyone else in his circle.

The Queen Mother had known "Dickie" Mountbatten for over 50 years. He had been a close friend of both her husband and the Duke of Windsor. She had so admired his courage during the war as a naval captain, as a brilliant commander-in-chief, and, after the war, as the last Viceroy of India before independence.

With the public, Lord Mountbatten was almost as popular as the Queen Mother, certainly in the later stages of his life. Like her, he was able to inspire, though his appeal sprang from being an extrovert, a natural and brilliant showman. The Queen Mother, even today, appears genuinely surprised that the public wish to make such a fuss of her. Lord Mountbatten would be surprised if they did not—and would do something about it if they did not! Her light and inspiration casts a warm, comforting glow over people. His was a spotlight that he shone on others as well as on himself. And when it went out it seemed as if not one light but a whole great battleship had suddenly been plunged into darkness.

Right: *The nation mourned a hero, the Royal Family mourned a relative and close friend*

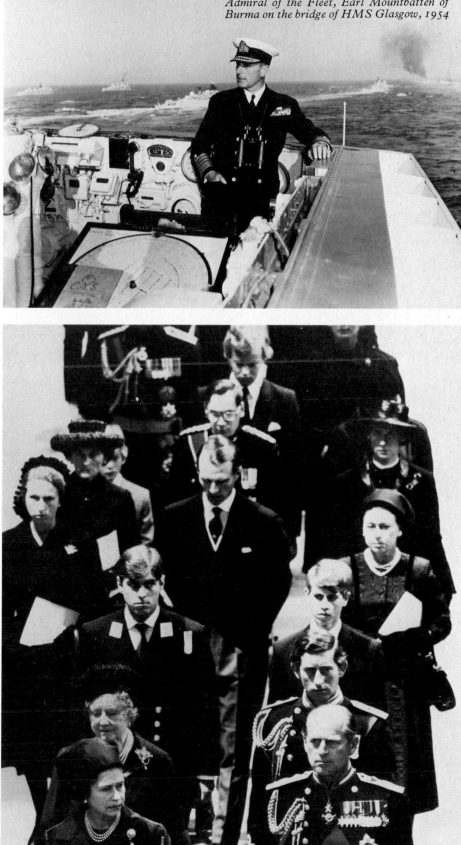

Admiral of the Fleet, Earl Mountbatten of Burma on the bridge of HMS Glasgow, 1954

In June and December...

1964

The Royal Family do not see nearly as much of one another as most people imagine. The Queen and Prince Charles lead their own lives, carry out their individual duties, even though they live in the same palace. Other members of the family may go months without seeing the Queen, except on television.

There are, however, two occasions in the year when by tradition as many as possible of the family come together. The first, in June, follows the Trooping the Colour ceremony when the Queen, splendid in crimson jacket and cockaded hat, steps on to the balcony of Buckingham Palace, followed by family and relations.

The other occasion is on Christmas Day, when everyone goes to morning service at St. George's Chapel, Windsor, and are photographed as they come out on to the steps afterwards. The pictures tell their own story of the passing years, the growing up of children, the arrival of additions to the Royal Family

1969

1975

1979

1969

1972

Over the years it has become a tradition for the Queen to entertain all the Royal Family at Windsor Castle over Christmas. On Christmas Day morning everyone attends family service at St. George's Chapel before going back to the Castle for the Christmas festivities, followed by the Queen's traditional televised greetings to the country and the Commonwealth

1974

1977

1979

Three generations of the Royal Family—rarely photographed together so informally. Queen Elizabeth, Queen Elizabeth the Queen Mother and Prince Charles, heir apparent to the Throne. The picture was taken outside the Royal Chapel, Windsor, 25 years to the day after the Queen's accession

Around the world in 80 years

1901

Queen Victoria dies

1902

Peace of Vereeniging ends Boer War.
Volcano erupts on Martinique —36,000 die

1903

Orville and Wilbur Wright make first powered flight

1904

Outbreak of Russo-Japanese War.
HMS Discovery returns after Antarctic expedition

1905

Japanese destroy Russian Baltic fleet.
Norway is declared independent from Sweden

1906

Emmeline Pankhurst launches militant campaign for women's suffrage

1907

New Zealand is granted Dominion status.
Robert Baden-Powell founds Boy Scout movement

1908

Herbert Asquith becomes British Prime Minister

1909

Louis Blériot makes first cross-Channel flight

1910

Labour Exchanges are established in Britain.
Florence Nightingale dies

1911

Norwegian explorer, Roald Amundsen, reaches South Pole

1912

SS Titanic strikes iceberg on maiden voyage—1,513 die

1913

News reaches Britain of Robert Scott's death 11 months before at South Pole

1914

The Great War begins.
First zeppelin appears over British coast

1915

Germans use gas warfare.
Douglas Haig takes over British command in France

1916

Lord Kitchener drowns

1917

Balfour Declaration recognises Palestine as a "national home" for Jews
Vladimir Lenin leads Bolsheviks in October Revolution in Russia

1918

Kaiser William II abdicates.
Armistice is signed

1919

Albert Einstein's theory of relativity is confirmed.
John Alcock and Arthur Brown make first non-stop flight across the Atlantic

1920

Prohibition comes into force in the USA

1921

Irish Free State is set up by peace treaty with Britain. Germany's war reparations bill is fixed at £6,650 million. Nearly 86 million working days are lost in Britain through strikes

1922

Benito Mussolini's Fascist movement marches on Rome

1923

Earthquake in Japan—Tokyo and Yokohama are in ruins. Gordon-Bennett balloon race ends in disaster

1924

Ramsay MacDonald forms first Labour government in Britain

1925

Summer Time Act is made permanent in Britain. Queen Alexandra dies

1926

General Strike in Britain lasts nine days. Germany asks to join League of Nations. Memorial Theatre in Stratford-on-Avon burns down

1927

Charles Lindbergh flies from New York to Paris in 37 hours

1928

Women in Britain win the vote. Earthquake in Greece destroys Corinth. Airship crosses Atlantic with 60 passengers

1929

Wall Street Crash—New York stock exchange collapses

1930

R101 airship crashes in France on first flight to India. Channel Tunnel scheme rejected by British Government

1931

Floods in China—4 million homes are destroyed. Resignation of Labour Government and formation of a coalition. Al Capone sentenced to 11 years' imprisonment

1932

Sydney Harbour Bridge opens. Serious rioting in Dartmoor Prison

1933

Adolf Hitler is appointed German Chancellor

1934

President Hindenburg dies— Hitler becomes dictator. The liner SS Queen Mary is launched

1935

Sir Malcolm Campbell breaks world land speed record in Bluebird at 301.337 m.p.h. Stanley Baldwin succeeds Ramsay MacDonald as British Prime Minister

1936

SS Queen Mary makes maiden voyage in record time to New York from Southampton. Civil War breaks out in Spain. Fred Perry wins men's singles championship for third time at Wimbledon

1937

London bus strike lasts 14 days. Sydney Wooderson sets new world record for running one mile in 4 minutes 6.6 seconds

1938

SS Queen Elizabeth—world's largest liner—is launched by Queen Elizabeth. Austria annexed by Germany. Munich agreement signed.

1939

Spanish Civil War ends— Britain recognises General Franco's government. World War II breaks out. Road deaths in Britain, largely due to "blackout", rise to 1,155 in one month

1940

Evacuation of Dunkirk—299 British warships and 420 other vessels rescue 335,490 men. Battle of Britain—1,733 German and 915 British planes are destroyed

1941

Nazi Rudolf Hess parachutes into Scotland.
Clothes rationing introduced in Britain.
Germany invades Greece, Yugoslavia and Russia.
Japanese attack Pearl Harbour

1942

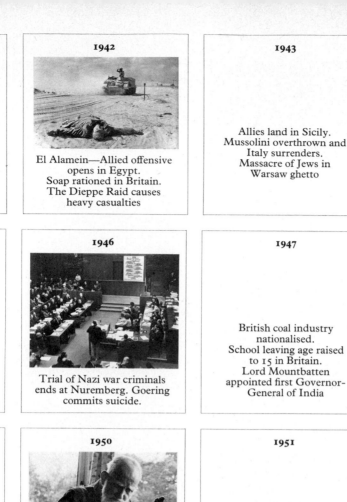

El Alamein—Allied offensive opens in Egypt.
Soap rationed in Britain.
The Dieppe Raid causes heavy casualties

1943

Allies land in Sicily.
Mussolini overthrown and Italy surrenders.
Massacre of Jews in Warsaw ghetto

1944

D-Day—June 6—Allied armies land in Normandy

1945

VE-Day—victory in Europe, May 8; VJ-Day—victory over Japan, September 2.
Hiroshima destroyed by first atomic bomb.
Clement Attlee wins general election in Britain

1946

Trial of Nazi war criminals ends at Nuremberg. Goering commits suicide.

1947

British coal industry nationalised.
School leaving age raised to 15 in Britain.
Lord Mountbatten appointed first Governor-General of India

1948

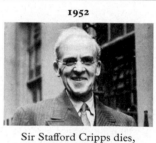

Mahatma Gandhi assassinated in New Delhi.
Russians force Berlin Airlift

1949

Gas industry nationalised.
Ten-power conference in London establishes Council of Europe. Mao Tse-Tung declares People's Republic of China

1950

George Bernard Shaw dies, aged 94.
Outbreak of Korean War

1951

General MacArthur relieved of all command in Far East.
Festival of Britain opened by King George VI.
Conservatives win British general election with small majority

1952

Sir Stafford Cripps dies, aged 63.
Britain's first atomic bomb test

1953

President Eisenhower becomes 34th President of USA.
Joseph Stalin dies, aged 74.
Edmund Hillary and Sherpa Tenzing reach summit of Mount Everest

1954

Roger Bannister becomes first man to run a mile in under four minutes.
Sir Winston Churchill celebrates 80th birthday

1955

Dr. Albert Einstein dies.
Revolt against Perón government in Argentina.
City of London becomes a "smokeless zone".
ITV begins broadcasting

1956

Colonel Nasser elected President of Egypt.
May is the driest month in Britain since 1896.
Russian troops suppress Hungarian uprising

1957

Sir Anthony Eden resigns over Suez crisis; Prime Minister Harold Macmillan succeeds him.
First Premium Bond prizes drawn by ERNIE.
First satellite launched by Russia

1958

Nikita Khrushchev elected to power in Russia.
General de Gaulle becomes President of France

1959

Fidel Castro overthrows Batista government in Cuba.
Jodrell Bank radios message to America via the moon.
First section of M1 motorway opens in Britain

1960

Aneurin Bevan dies, aged 62.
John Kennedy elected President of USA

1961

Sir Thomas Beecham dies.
Major Yuri Gagarin makes first manned flight into space.
Betting shops open in Britain

1962

Marilyn Monroe dies, aged 36.
Britain's first communications satellite launched

1963

Harold Wilson becomes leader of Labour Party.
£2·5 million stolen in Great Train Robbery.
President Kennedy assassinated in Dallas, Texas

1964

Harold Wilson becomes Labour Prime Minister.
BBC2 Television opens

1965

Sir Winston Churchill dies, aged 90.
American aircraft bomb North Vietnam.
Ian Smith makes Rhodesian Declaration of Independence

1966

England wins World Cup at Wembley.
Aberfan colliery tip disaster—116 children killed

1967

Donald Campbell killed trying to beat water speed record on Lake Coniston.
Six-day war breaks out in Middle East.
First human heart transplant is performed in Cape Town

1968

Senator Robert Kennedy assassinated in Los Angeles.
Russian forces invade Czechoslovakia

1969

Maiden flight of Concorde.
British Army guard key points in Northern Ireland.
Neil Armstrong and Edwin Aldrin are first men to land on the moon

1970

General de Gaulle dies, aged 79.
Damages awarded to 28 deformed Thalidomide children

1971

Open University goes on the air in Britain.
Britain "goes decimal".
Louis Armstrong dies.
Internment without trial introduced in Northern Ireland

1972

Seven killed in IRA bomb explosion at Aldershot.
Five burglars caught in Watergate building, Washington DC

1973

Britain, Ireland and Denmark join the EEC.
Last American soldiers leave Vietnam.
VAT introduced in Britain

1974

President Nixon resigns over Watergate scandal.
Edward Heath resigns, minority Labour government takes office

1975

Mrs. Margaret Thatcher elected leader of Conservative Party.
Moorgate tube crash—41 die.
Referendum held on Common Market—2 to 1 majority in favour of staying in

1976

Idi Amin declares himself President of Uganda for life.
Harold Wilson resigns; James Callaghan takes over.
Jimmy Carter elected President of USA

1977

Indian Prime Minister, Mrs. Indira Gandhi, resigns.
Maria Callas dies.
Bing Crosby dies.
Freddie Laker opens Skytrain service to New York

1978

Cardinal Karol Wojtyla of Poland becomes first non-Italian Pope for 450 years.
346 Vietnamese "boat people" arrive in Britain

1979

The Shah of Iran leaves the country and Ayatollah Khomeini returns from exile.
British MP, Airey Neave, assassinated.
Margaret Thatcher becomes first woman Prime Minister

1980

Controversy surrounds Moscow Olympics.
Iranian crisis threatens another world war

Photographic Contributors

Associated Newspapers; Associated Press; Marcus Adams; Baron; BBC
Hulton Picture Library; Cecil Beaton; Camera Press; Henry M. Carter;
Central Press; Peter Cheze-Brown; Country Life Books; Daily
Telegraph; Fox Photos; Glasgow Herald; Lord Adam Gordon;
Tim Graham; Greater London Council Architects; Anwar Hussein;
Illustrated London News Picture Library; Keystone Press; Patrick
Lichfield; Studio Lisa; Movietone Film Archive; By courtesy of the
National Portrait Gallery, London; Norman Parkinson; Paul Popper;
Press Association; Rex Features; Royal College of Music; Royal
Photographic Society/Kodak; Scots News; John Scott/OPFA;
Snowdon; Spectrum Colour Library; A. V. Swaebe; Syndication
International; The Times; Topix; Royal College of Physicians of
Edinburgh; UPI; Reproduced by gracious permission of Her Majesty
the Queen

Bibliography

Mabel, Countess of Airlie: Thatched with Gold (Hutchinson); Helen
Cathcart: The Queen Mother Herself (W. H. Allen); Marion Crawford:
The Little Princesses (Cassell); W. E. Shewell-Cooper: The Royal
Gardeners—King George VI and His Queen (Cassell); Frances
Donaldson: Edward VIII (Weidenfeld and Nicolson); Norman
Hartnell: Silver and Gold (Evans); Ivor Herbert: The Queen Mother's
Horses (Pelham); Christopher Hibbert: The Court at Windsor—A
Domestic History (Longman); Robert Lacey: Majesty (Hutchinson);
Dorothy Laird: Queen Elizabeth the Queen Mother (Hodder and
Stoughton); John Montgomery: Royal Dogs (Max Parrish); Dermot
Morrah: To Be a King (Hutchinson); Sally Patience: The Queen
Mother (Lutterworth Press); Eleanor Roosevelt: This I Remember
(Hutchinson); Godfrey Talbot: The Country Life Book of Queen
Elizabeth the Queen Mother (Country Life Books); Peter Townsend:
Time and Chance (Collins); Sir John Wheeler-Bennett: King George
VI, His Life and Reign (Macmillan); The Duchess of Windsor: The
Heart has its Reasons (Michael Joseph); HRH The Duke of Windsor: A
King's Story (Cassell)

CONDITIONS OF SALE AND SUPPLY:
This publication is sold subject to the following conditions, namely that it shall not, without the written consent of the publishers first given, be lent, resold, hired out or otherwise disposed of by way of Trade at a price in excess of the recommended maximum price shown on the frontispiece (selling price in Eire subject to VAT); and that it shall not be lent, resold, hired out or otherwise disposed of in a mutilated condition or in any unauthorised cover by way of Trade; or affixed to or as part of any publication or advertising, literary or pictorial matter whatsoever.